ESSAYS IN
SUPPLY SIDE ECONOMICS

Edited by David G. Raboy

With a Foreword by Edwin J. Feulner, Jr.

HB
241
.E847
1982

© Copyright February 1982
by
The Institute for Research on the Economics of Taxation
Washington, D.C.

Acknowledgement

I would like to thank Lauren Cook, Susan Schaeffer, Michael Schuyler, Steven Lagerfeld and John Von Kannon, who helped to make the publication of this book possible.

TABLE OF CONTENTS

Foreword
Edwin J. Feulner, Jr.
1

Introduction
David G. Raboy
3

Supply Side Analysis and Public Policy
Norman B. Ture
7

The Theoretical Heritage of Supply Side Economics
David G. Raboy
29

Rational Expectations and Supply Side Economics: Match or Mismatch?
David G. Tuerck
63

The Enterprise System, Democracy, and the General Welfare: An Approach to Reconciliation
Richard E. Wagner
93

Taxation, Savings, and Labor Supply: Theory and Evidence of Distortions
Mai Nguyen Woo
119

From Antitrust to Supply-Side Economics: The Strange History of Federal Intervention in the Economy
Naomi R. Lamoreaux
151

Foreword

SUPPLY SIDE ECONOMICS, AS EMBODIED IN THE ECONOMIC Recovery Tax Act of 1981, has become the most widely discussed economic theory to emerge in several decades; it has also been largely misunderstood and maligned. This important collection of essays puts to rest many of the popular misconceptions that have been expressed by the press, policy-makers, and the public concerning the legitimacy of supply side economics and the implications of the Reagan administration's economic policies.

For many years, policy makers operated on the false assumption that government policy could not affect conditions of supply, and that economic fine-tuning could successfully be achieved on the demand side. This led to policies of government intervention, primarily in the form of government spending. But, spending policies have only proven that the government can and does affect conditions of supply; that government spending and taxing policies can and have severely restricted producers' abilities and incentives to supply goods and services. The growing conviction that interventionist policies have retarded real growth in our economy culminated in the election of Ronald Reagan and in wide support of the Economic Recovery Tax Act.

Given the political success of the Tax Act of 1981, and all of the attention accorded the debates in Congress on the act, one could have acquired the misconception that supply side economics is a political movement with little or no economic theory behind it. Indeed, the popularity of supply side policies, and the conviction that they will work, is for most people a matter of intuitive knowledge. Heretofore there existed no comprehensive explanation of supply side economic theory or of the evidence that policies based on supply side economics will work; this volume supplies that explanation. For this reason these essays will be most important to legislators, the administration, the academic and business communities, and to all individuals who wish to understand the future course of economic policy.

Edwin J. Feulner, Jr., Ph.D.

Introduction

THE PAST YEAR BROUGHT A DRAMATIC TURNAROUND IN GOVernment economic policy. But many people found themselves frustrated in their attempts to find sources that logically and consistently explained the theories behind the new direction in policy. The popular press offered little help. It seized on some of the more bizarre ideas promoted on the fringes of the debate, leaving a void where a proper definition of the new supply side economics belonged.

The purpose of this volume is to offer such a definition — to address the key theoretical, empirical, and policy aspects of the economic thought which has so profoundly influenced the policies of the federal government.

Probably the single most important question concerns the basic analytics of supply side economics: How does the theory treat government taxing and spending policies and the way in which they impact upon the economy? Certainly no one is more qualified to comment on that subject than Norman B. Ture, one of the foremost supply side theoreticians. Dr. Ture is a past president of IRET and currently serves as Under Secretary of the Treasury for Tax and Economic Affairs. In his essay, "Supply Side Analysis and Public Policy," he stresses the role of changing relative costs and prices in determining the effects of government activity. A careful reading of Dr. Ture's essay will give the reader a good understanding of the fundamentals of supply side economics.

My contribution is "The Theoretical Heritage of Supply Side Economics," in which I dispute the mutually contradictory claims that supply side economics has no theoretical underpinnings and that the theories are untested. I trace the development of free market economics from Adam Smith to the present, demonstrating that supply side economics is the outcome of over two hundred years of evolving economic thought.

The third essay explores the relationship between supply side economics and recent developments in monetarism. The popular press has drawn a false distinction between the neoclassical school of monetary theory (monetarism) and the neoclassical school of public finance (supply side economics), ignoring the intellectual kinship between the two. Those ties are particularly strong in the case of the "new classical" or "rational expectations" school that has evolved within the monetarist camp. In rational expectations theory, it is assumed that individuals are fully cognizant of the real effects of government activity and adjust their decision-making according to their expectations of government actions. In "Rational Expectations and Supply Side Economics: Match or Mismatch?" Dr. David Tuerck discusses the evolution of the rational expectations school as an intellectually satisfying response to Keynesian "money illusion" and considers the extent to which rational expectations are embodied in supply side theories.

One of the driving forces behind the Reagan economic program was the belief that government had grown too large. Most economists would agree that some justification for government in the economy exists, given that the market fails in certain instances to allocate resources efficiently. Yet, it is clear that the government has over-reacted to this phenomenon in the past and has often failed to adopt the most cost-effective means of correcting for "market failures." In "The Enterprise System, Democracy, and the General Welfare: An Approach to Reconciliation," Richard Wagner addresses a variety of important issues in public economics. First, Professor Wagner considers the nature of market failures and shows how the market mechanism can be used to internalize these failures. Secondly, he examines different democratic structures and shows why a simple majority system may result in excessive government intervention in the economy and, ultimately, destructive inefficiency. His suggestions about how to avoid super-optimal government expenditures are particularly provocative and timely.

Two of the most hotly debated topics during the economic policy debates of the past year were the responsiveness of saving and work effort to tax treatment. "Taxation, Saving, and Labor Supply: Theory and Evidence of Distortions" by Mai Woo surveys the theoretical and empirical evidence on the effects of taxation on the labor/leisure and save/consume decisions. Pointing out that a pure income tax system distorts both of these decisions, Dr. Woo goes on to analyze today's hybrid tax system, revealing the inefficiencies produced by its creation of opportunities for tax arbitrage. She also looks at the distortions caused by a tax system that was not designed for today's inflationary economy. Finally, Dr. Woo argues that given these three problems of the current tax system, a progressive consumption tax would be the best alternative because of its greater neutrality.

Supply side economics is primarily concerned with the role of government within a market system. In the final essay, "From Antitrust to Supply Side Economics: The Strange History of Federal Intervention in the Economy," Naomi Lamoreaux traces the history of public opinion on this issue through all its dramatic changes, from the nineteenth century to the present. A popular consensus for smaller government does exist today, Professor Lamoreaux concludes, and she also has some interesting and original things to say about Herbert Hoover, Franklin D. Roosevelt, and Jimmy Carter, as well as Ronald Reagan.

—David G. Raboy
February 1, 1982

SUPPLY SIDE ANALYSIS AND PUBLIC POLICY

by

NORMAN B. TURE

Norman B. Ture is Under Secretary of the Treasury for Tax and Economic Affairs and former president of the Institute for Research on the Economics of Taxation and Norman B. Ture, Inc. This paper was written while Dr. Ture was president of IRET and its publication was made possible by a grant from the Manhattan Institute for Policy Research.

Introduction: The Emergence of Supply Side Policies

SELDOM HAS A SET OF IDEAS SO CAPTURED THE THINKING OF policy makers and so dramatically altered policy prescriptions as has the so-called supply side economics in the last few years. To be sure, the concepts comprising supply side analysis and distinguishing it from a more conventional approach to public economic policy are not well understood by all, or even most, of its devotees, but its policy thrust is more widely accepted with every passing day. And despite its conceptual origins in the neoclassical theoretical traditions, hence, one might presume, its affinity for political conservatives, its policy applications have gained acceptance across virtually the entire spectrum of political positions. And all of this has occurred in less than half a decade—indeed since Congressman Jack Kemp first presented the supply side approach in connection with his Jobs Creation Act in 1975.

In the popular view, supply side economics appears to call for a focus of public policy on augmenting supplies of privately-provided productive services, hence the supply of output, in lieu of concentrating on aggregate demand. It is this aspect of supply side economics which probably accounts, for the most part, for its meteoric rise in popularity among policy makers. For roughly four decades, public economic policy in much of the western world, certainly in the United States, was guided by prescriptions derived, more or less rigorously, from *The General Theory of Employment, Interest, and Money* by John Maynard Keynes. In oversimplified terms, the Keynesian prescripts hold that unsatisfactory aggregate economic performance results from insufficient or excessive aggregate demand, i.e., the sum of the total spending by households for consumption goods and services plus the aggregate outlays by business for capital instruments of all sorts plus governments' purchases of goods and services. In the (oversimplified) Keynesian scenario, the conditions of supply are given, to all intents and purposes, in the short term and are substantially unresponsive to public policy in the long run. In other words, the Keynesian analysis doesn't deny or ignore conditions of supply but rather treats them as determined by factors lying beyond the reach of public policy. To influence aggregate economic outcomes, therefore, the policy focus in the Keynesian approach is necessarily on aggregate demand. If there are apparently idle human and capital resources, public policy should augment aggregate demand until inflationary pressures emerge (i.e., until the aggregate supply curve begins to tilt upward from its horizontal position). If there is an unacceptable rate of inflation, aggregate demand must be depressed, implying a decrease in employment and output along with the decline in the price level (or more realistically its rate of increase).

This deeply entrenched view of an inherent trade-off between employment and output gain, on the one hand, and inflation containment, on the other, formalized in the Phillips curve, may well have afforded the springboard for the ready acceptance of the supply side view of things. Inflation, at varying rates, all of them unacceptably high, plagued the economy throughout the 1970s while unemployment persisted in the range of about 5 percent to about 8.5 percent and gains in productivity, output, and real income slowed, particularly in the last half of the decade. The coincidence of high unemployment and low output gains with high inflation urged either that there is in fact no necessary trade-off or that the trade can be made only at an extremely high unemployment rate. If the Keynesian view of things were to guide public policy, policy makers would face an impossible decision between accepting even higher unemployment rates to bring inflation down well below the double-digit rate of 1979 or accepting even higher double-digit inflation rates to get unemployment down to the 4 percent rate mandated in the Humphrey-Hawkins Act. No wonder wage and price controls appeared so alluring, despite their repeated failure to do anything but misallocate resources and create scarcities.

In this context there emerged a view which seemed to afford a way of breaking out of the dilemma. The supply side prescriptions called for restricting the growth in nominal aggregate demand by curtailing the expansion of government spending and by slowing the rate of increase in the stock of money while removing or mitigating tax disincentives for market-oriented effort and for saving and capital formation. This set of policies would, so it is argued, both expand employment and output and reduce inflation.

The signal feature of this policy approach is that it rejects the view that reducing the level — or rate of increase — of nominal aggregate demand necessarily results in a reduction in employment and output; in fact, it asserts that constraining the growth in nominal demand facilitates the growth in employment, output, and real income.

The principal impetus for accelerating the growth in real economic magnitudes, however, is seen as coming from easing the barriers thereto erected by the existing tax system.

The timing of the supply side policy prescription surely must have had much to do with the startlingly rapid pace of its acceptance. (On the other hand, the circumstances which led to so ready and eager an embrace of supply side economics must have been important factors in bringing these views and policy prescriptions forward in the policy forum.) As all too frequently happens under these conditions, enthusiasm for the supply side policies was sometimes inadequately constrained by careful reasoning; some proponents were inclined to claim too much. One of these excessive claims is that supply side tax reductions will so expand GNP as to generate larger tax revenues than will be realized without the tax cuts. This sort of fiscal alchemy elicited derision from many economists and policy-makers; fortunately, it has not diverted key participants in the policy forum from pursuit of supply side policies.[1] It has, however, misdirected much of the discussion about supply side economics.

Basic Concepts of Supply Side Economics

There have, to date, been few serious efforts to delineate the basic propositions which comprise supply side economics. This neglect is regrettable, since it has allowed die-hard critics of the policy positions which are derived from the supply side analysis to pin a snake-oil label on both the analysis and the policies. In fact, supply side economics affords no magical nostrums. Nor is it properly perceived as a new and revolutionary general theory.

Supply side economics is merely the application of price theory—so-called "microeconomics"—in the analysis of problems concerning economic aggregates—so-called "macroeconomics." Its conceptual antecedents are to be found in the work of the classical economists of the modern era from Adam Smith and J. B. Say through Milton Friedman and Gary Becker. As such, it presents no new body of theory; rather it entails addressing the neoclassical mode of analysis to public economic policies, whether these are focused on concerns of the economy as a whole or of particular groups therein.

---

[1] Nothing in the basic supply side analysis holds that tax cuts so expand output and income, hence tax bases, as to provide more revenue than would otherwise be generated. On the other hand, the supply side analysis can and does identify certain types of tax reductions which, in fact, are net tax revenue producers rather than losers. One such type of tax change consists of tax reductions which lie in the future but positively affect saving and investment behavior in the present in anticipation of reduced taxes on the future returns on the saving.

First-order price effects

The basic and distinctive characteristic of supply side economics is that it identifies the *initial* effect of government actions in terms of the changes in relative prices (explicit or implicit) confronting households and businesses which these actions entail. It is the response by these private sector entities to these relative price changes which determines the ultimate effects of the government actions. These responses involve changes in the allocation of existing production resources and claims on output which may result, more or less promptly, in changes in the total volume and/or composition of economic activity. Insofar as volume changes occur, aggregate real income is also changed, and this change in total real income will lead to further changes in economic activity. Since real aggregate demand is necessarily always equal to aggregate real income, these further changes in economic activity may be conveniently measured in terms of changes in the components of aggregate demand. This sequence of effects—the precedence of price over income effects—is one of the critically important premises of the supply side analysis. In a technical short-hand, the effect of government activities on relative prices is the "first-order" effect and the consequences of private-sector responses thereto for total income is the "second-order" effect.

Equivalently, the supply side analysis points out that government actions first affect the allocation of resources and that one of the consequences of any such allocative effect may be a change in the level of aggregate economic activity. This mode of analysis similarly holds that these allocative effects of fiscal actions also largely determine the distributional consequences of fiscal action.[2]

The basic supply side proposition denies the possibility that government action can initially and directly change the total real income of the economy. This denial of first-order income effects, the critically distinguishing feature of the supply side analysis, is the major obstacle to its acceptance. We have all been conditioned for ages past to look to the effects of tax changes on our disposable incomes and to perceive changes in government spending totals as directly increasing or reducing aggregate demand. And through all the sharp divergences in monetary theory, there runs a consensus that changes in monetary aggregates directly affect real output, at least in the short run. The challenge posed by supply side theory, therefore, is a substantial one.

---

[2] To appreciate the importance of this set of propositions, bear in mind that for several decades past the conventional wisdom has held that diverse public policies separately and independently determine the allocation of resources, the distribution of income and wealth, and the rate of increase in total economic activity, in both nominal and real terms.

The prevailing view that government actions do directly affect aggregate income derives from perceiving these actions as impacting initially and directly on aggregate demand, via effects on disposable income, the changes in which are deemed to result directly in changes in total production. The supply side analysis, on the other hand, holds that government actions have no direct initial impact on *real* aggregate demand and, indeed, affect nominal aggregate demand only as a consequence of changes in the stock of money. Changes in *real* aggregate demand, to be sure, would elicit increases in total output. The pertinent question is how changes in real aggregate demand can occur without a preceding change in total output. By definition, aggregate demand is the sum of purchases of all types by all economic entities—governments, businesses, households, etc. Also by definition, these outlays must exactly equal aggregate income which in turn, at every moment in time, must just equal the value of aggregate output. Changes in real income, therefore, occur only as changes in output occur. And changes in output occur only as a result of changes in the amount of production inputs or in the intensity or efficiency of their use. To have a first-order effect on income, therefore, government actions would have to alter directly the amount or effectiveness of production inputs committed to production. But government actions, in and of themselves, do not change the aggregate amount of production resources available in the economy or their productivity. Changes in the amount of production inputs committed to production will result only if the real rewards for their use, i.e., the real price received per unit of input, is changed.[3]

To assume the contrary requires one to believe that the opportunity costs for providing more labor or capital services are constant in the short run, i.e., that short-run supply curves are horizontal or infinitely price elastic. Clearly, an increase in nominal, rather than real, aggregate demand resulting from government action could elicit an increase in real output, hence real total income and real total demand, only if suppliers of production inputs mistake increases in nominal for increases in real rewards for these inputs.

To illustrate, assume that the government's budget is balanced at the outset and that taxes are then reduced without any reduction in government spending. Also assume that the fiscal change impels no change in the stock of money. The initial effect, in the conventional aggregate demand approach, is identified as an increase in disposable income which results in an increase in total private sector

---

[3] Changes in the effectiveness with which inputs are used may result directly from government actions which reallocate these inputs among private and public sector uses.

spending, principally for consumption. But no such increase in total private sector spending in fact can occur.

Since the tax cut, by assumption, is not matched by a government spending cut, the loss in tax revenues—which is just equal to the increase in disposable income—must result in an equal deficit.

In real terms, as measured in conventional national income accounting, aggregate saving, at this point, is reduced. But since the deficit *must* be financed by saving, either *saving* must increase in an amount equal to the increase in disposable income and the deficit, by assumption precluding any increase in consumption spending, or investment must decrease in an amount equal to the deficit. (To digress for a moment, this latter alternative is the conventional perception of the "crowding out" phenomenon, i.e., government deficits displace private capital formation. This perception is at odds with contemporary theory about the determinants of investment. In highly abbreviated and oversimplified terms, investment is the process of adjusting the stock of capital from a former to a new optimum amount—or growth path—where the optimum amount depends on aggregate endowments, hence the marginal utility of an increment of income, and the opportunity cost—the amount of current consumption which must be foregone—to obtain any increment of income from capital. In this context, a government deficit would be relevant to the investment decision—would result in an equal decrease in investment—only if the deficit were perceived as entailing subsequent increases in the taxes on the future income stream to be produced by capital.) In either case, whether consumption or investment falls in an amount equal to the deficit, it is clear that no change in aggregate spending can occur as the initial effect of the tax reduction. If some people use their additional disposable income to finance additional spending for goods and services, then others will have to reduce their spending. Some redistribution of spending will occur in this case, but there is no increase in the total amount.

This rejection of an aggregate demand effect of a tax reduction does not mean that all tax reductions are perceived by the supply-side analyst to be inconsequential. On the contrary, since virtually every tax has some excise effect—alters the cost of something relative to the cost of other things—virtually every tax reduction will impel some response in the form of a change in the composition in the demands for the use of resources and in their allocation among their alternative use. A tax reduction which reduces the cost of market-oriented effort relative to "leisure" uses of one's time and resources will result in an increase in the supply of labor services, and other things equal, in an increase in real output, real income, hence aggregate real spending. It is not the effect of the tax cut on the deficit which generates this result but the effects on the relative costs of work and leisure. Similarly, a tax reduction which reduces the cost of saving relative to consumption will lead to an increase in the supply of capital services, hence to an increase in output, real income, and real spending. In either case, the magnitude of the effect on real output and spending is not a function of the size of the deficit but of the nature of the tax cut and the magnitude of its effect on the respective relative costs of efforts and of saving.

Consider next an alternative expansionary fiscal action—holding taxes constant while increasing government outlays. Suppose first the increased spending is in the form of transfer payments, i.e., involves no direct increase in government demand for goods or services. As in the case of tax reductions, those whose disposable incomes are increased—the recipients of the additional transfer payments—may well seek to add to their total outlays, but others must reduce their spending and purchase the additional government debt instruments. The identity of the spending and the composition of the spending may well change, but the aggregate amount of real spending cannot, at the outset, be altered.

Suppose the increase in government outlays takes the form of purchases of goods or services. Parallel to the prior cases, these additional outlays cannot be deemed to expand aggregate demand since the matching deficit they generate must be financed in real terms by a decrease in private spending. Nor should the additional outlays be thought to increase the real or effective demand for production inputs, hence, to increase aggregate employment, output, and income. To repeat an earlier observation, only if the opportunity costs for providing more production inputs are constant in the short run—only if short-run factor supply curves are horizontal or infinitely price elastic—would an increase in nominal government demand for outputs or production inputs result in increases in total output. In the real world, government spending in the form of purchases of goods and services alters (explicit or implicit) relative prices by changing the composition of aggregate demand. Government purchases of any given product or service initially increase the nominal demand for those products, hence for the production inputs their output entails. This change in demand per se must increase the nominal price of the products or services, compared to the prices at which they would otherwise sell in the private sector. The consequence of this price distortion is a reduction in private sector purchases of these goods and services. The increase in the direct or derived demand for the particular inputs raises the market price faced by private sector purchasers of these inputs, hence reduces private sector purchases, thereby shifting their use from private sector to government sector outputs.

These changes in demand resulting from government purchases

do not *per se* entail any change in the productivity of the production inputs involved. The real rate of return for any given quantity of any such input is, therefore, not altered. By the same token, the supply of the production inputs is not increased, although the allocation clearly is changed. No change in aggregate output, accordingly, results on this score from the government purchases.

The reallocation of production inputs, on the other hand, may result in a change in total real output if the real productivity on the inputs is enhanced or diminished in the government's, as opposed to the private sector's, use. A change in the amount of government purchases does not change total output and income by altering aggregate demand; any such change in real total income results only from changes in the effectiveness with which the production inputs are used. Changes in total output of this sort, obviously, need not be positively correlated with the amount of government purchases.

Finally, consider a monetary expansion, whether or not associated with an increase in the government's deficit. In the supply side analysis, an increase in the stock of money implies an increase in nominal income but no corresponding increase in output and real income. As the preceding discussion urges, any expansion of real output depends on an increase in the amount of production inputs (or in the efficiency of their use). In turn, this depends on an increase in the real rewards for supplying these inputs. But monetary expansion *per se* affords no increase in these real rewards, hence does not lead directly to an increase in the amount of inputs supplied nor, accordingly, to an increase in output. The expansion of nominal income resulting from an increase in the stock of money, therefore, reflects only an increase in the price level.

Policy Implications

This insistence on assigning first-order price effects to government action and on treating income effects as secondary in sequence—not in magnitude—is not a matter merely of abstract theoretical interest. Its implications for the practical aspects of public economic policy are enormous. At the outset, it requires identification of the way in which government actions affect relative prices.

Price effects of the tax system

First-order relative price effects are best illustrated in the case of tax policy. Every tax has the attribute of altering relative prices or costs. This is obvious in the case of selective excises: an excise on gasoline is seen by virtually everyone as raising the price the motorist must pay for gasoline compared with prices he or she must pay for other things. This price or cost effect, however, is not limited to those taxes we call excises. Every tax has some "excise effect." A perfectly neutral tax, if one could be devised, would have no excise effect; it would increase in the same proportion all of the prices confronting any entity in the private sector. It would increase the cost of effort in the same proportion as the cost of leisure, of saving in the same proportion as the cost of consumption, of any one consumption good or service in the same proportion as all others, of using labor services in the same proportion as capital services, of any one kind of labor or capital service in the same proportion as any other, etc.

The present tax system very thoroughly violates this neutrality criterion. It imposes severe excises on effort and on saving, along with a host of differential excises on various types of labor services and various forms of capital income.

Payroll and income taxes fall on the returns for "effort"—the use of labor services to produce goods and services exchanged in the markets; these taxes are not generally imposed on the rewards for "leisure"—the use of one's time and resources in nonmarket activities for which no explicit measure of income is afforded.

Since income generated by effort is subject to payroll and income taxes whereas that produced in leisure activities is not, these taxes must raise the cost of the former relative to the cost of the latter.[4]

With 24 hours per day it is clear that for each hour in which one uses one's resources for effort there is an hour less of leisure available. The cost of a marginal hour of effort, then, is the value of the hour of leisure which must be foregone. For example, suppose a person were to earn $10 an hour in a particular job. Each hour the person could spend on the job but chooses instead to spend in leisure costs him or her $10. To optimize the person would allocate time between the two alternatives such that the value of the rewards for the last hour of leisure was just equal to $10. Then the marginal cost of the effort to the person is $10, the value of the foregone leisure; similarly, the marginal cost of leisure is $10, the foregone reward for effort. The cost of effort relative to the cost of leisure—the ratio of these costs—is 1:1.

A tax which is levied on the explicit rewards for effort but not on the returns for leisure uses of one's time clearly increases the cost of the former relative to the latter. For example, at a marginal rate of

---

[4] The concept of cost that is relevant for this purpose, as in the case of economic analysis generally, is that of opportunity cost—the value of that which must be foregone in using production resources in a particular way. The concept derives its pertinence from the rudimentary facts of economic life that production resources are scarce relative to the wants they may be used to satisfy and that with relatively few exceptions, the use of given quantities of given resources to produce particular outputs excludes their production of other outputs in that same period of time.

25 percent, an income tax raises the marginal cost of effort by a third relative to leisure and equivalently, reduces the marginal cost of leisure by 25 percent relative to effort.[5]

The excise effect on effort in the income tax is greater the higher the marginal rate of tax. A 50 percent marginal tax rate, for example, doubles the cost of effort relative to leisure. A graduated or progressive income tax, therefore, enhances this excise effect. On the appealing assumption that, for the most part, the higher the rate of compensation for effort the more productive the effort is, a graduated income tax increases the cost of effort relative to leisure more the more productive the effort. By the same token, graduation raises the cost of increasing one's productivity.

In the same vein, but perhaps not so obviously, the present tax system raises the cost of saving relative to the cost of current consumption. Just as effort and leisure exhaust one's available time, saving and consumption exhaust one's available income. The cost of saving a part of one's income, then, is the amount of current consumption that one must forego. Similarly, the cost of using part of one's income for current consumption is the amount of saving given up. Since saving is the purchase of a future income stream, the cost of any given amount of consumption is the future income which one must forego. An income tax of the sort levied in the United States raises the cost of saving relative to consumption, and this inherent income tax bias is accentuated by graduation and by the piling on of multiple layers of tax on the same income stream representing the returns on saving.

For example, suppose that with no tax one might use a marginal $1,000 of income to buy $1,000 worth of consumption goods and services now or buy an asset, say a bond, which at an interest rate of 10 percent, will produce $100 a year forever. Clearly, the cost of the $1,000 of additional current consumption is the foregone $100 per year; by the same token, the cost of an additional $100 of income every year is $1,000 of foregone current consumption.

With an income tax, the terms of this trade-off between current consumption and future income are altered. Again suppose one's marginal tax rate is 25 percent. Then one's marginal $1,000 of in-

---

[5] With the 25 percent marginal tax rate, the net reward for an hour's effort is $7.50—the amount of the hourly wage left after paying the tax. The marginal cost of an hour's leisure falls, therefore, from $10.00 to $7.50, while the marginal cost of an hour's effort—the value of the foregone leisure—remains at $10.00, in absolute terms. The cost of leisure relative to the cost of effort becomes $\frac{7.50}{10.00} = .75$, and the cost of effort relative to the cost of leisure becomes $\frac{10.00}{7.50} = 1.33$.

come is reduced by the tax to $750, with which one can buy $750 of consumption goods and services now or a future income stream of $75.00 per year, assuming the interest rate remains at 10 percent. But the $75.00 of future income will also be subject to income tax, let us assume at the same marginal rate of 25 percent. Then the net-of-tax future income is $56.25. Before the tax was imposed, one had to give up $1,000 of current consumption to obtain $100 per year of additional income; the marginal cost per dollar of future income was $10. With the tax, one must forego $750 of current consumption to obtain $56.25 of additional income per year; the marginal cost with the tax is $13.33 per dollar of future income. The 25 percent income tax increases the cost of future income relative to current consumption by 33 ⅓ percent.[6]

With graduation of income tax rates, the tax increases the cost of future income relative to consumption more than in proportion to the amount and/or productivity of saving. Since the marginal tax rate depends in large part on the amount of one's income, and since the amount of one's current income is likely to reflect in some part the amount one has saved in the past, the excise effect of the tax on saving is likely to be greater the greater the amount one saves. Similarly, the greater the return per dollar of saving—the more productive one's saving—the higher is likely to be the marginal tax rate and, therefore, the greater the cost of additional saving relative to additional consumption.

To an even greater extent than in the case of the effort-leisure trade-off, the existing tax system is biased against saving and in favor of consumption. The basic bias, as shown, derives from the fact that the individual income tax is levied both on the amount saved and on the future income generated by the saving. But severe as this tax penalty itself may be, it is only the base of a pyramid of taxes resting on the same income stream. In the federal tax system, the corporation income tax constitutes another major tier of taxes on the returns to individuals' saving. The amount an individual saves is taxed as part of his current income, as shown above. If the saving takes the form of purchase of corporate stocks, the returns on the

---

[6] An equivalent way of looking at this effect is that prior to the tax, with an interest rate of 10 percent, the capitalized value of the $100 per year of additional income is $1,000 $(= \frac{\$100}{.10})$. With the income tax, the capitalized value of the after-tax additional income per year is 562.50 $(= \frac{\$56.25}{.10})$. Before the tax, the ratio of the marginal outlay on consumption to the present worth of the future income is $1,000:$1,000 = 1$; with the tax, the ratio becomes $750:$562.50 = 1.333$. The cost of future income relative to the cost of consumption increases by one-third; equivalently, the cost of consumption relative to saving falls by 25 percent.

saving will be taxed initially under the corporate income tax. Insofar as the corporation pays dividends to the individual saver-shareholder, the individual pays tax again, further reducing the return to him per dollar of saving.

Another layer of tax on the returns to saving is provided by the tax on capital gains. A capital gain is the market's capitalization of an increase in the expected future income attributable to an asset. In an efficient market, corporate retained earnings will be reflected in increases in the market value of the company's shares. This capital gain, obviously, is the capitalized value of the expected increase in earnings per share generated by the investment of the retained earnings. Imposing a tax on the gains realized if the shares are sold or exchanged is to lay an additional "one-shot" tax on the same stream of future income which the shareholder bought with the initial investment.

The source of the capital gain is the amount of earnings retained after the corporate tax was paid. At the time the gain is realized, it is the capitalized value of the expected increase in future earnings, which will in turn be taxed as they accrue. The tax on capital gains, thus, is an *additional* levy on an income stream subject to several layers of tax in any event.

The same returns on saving are also subject to the income taxes imposed by all but a few of the states. And insofar as the saving takes the form of real property, the same income stream is likely to be subject to state and local government property taxes, which though levied on the assessed value of the assets may be usefully perceived as imposts on the explicit or imputed income they generate.

Federal and state taxes on property transfers by gift or at death are akin to capital gains taxes with respect to their effects on the cost of future income compared with present consumption. The base of such taxes is the market value of the transferred property, which in turn equals the present value of the future income the property is expected to produce. That future income will, in the ordinary course of events, be taxed as it materializes over time. Taxing its capitalized amount on the occasion of the property transfer is an additional levy on the same income stream.

Moreover, the property may also be perceived as the accumulated amount of past income which had been reserved from consumption. Again, in the ordinary course of events, that past income had been taxed as it was received. Taxes on the value of the property on the occasion of its transfer are a further layer of tax on the same income stream.[7]

---

[7] The extra burden on saving of these transfer taxes is mitigated by the various tax provisions which reduce the taxable amount of the property. It is also moderated by the fact that for

The tax laws, particularly the income taxes, contain numerous provisions which somewhat ameliorate the effects of the multiple layers of tax on the rewards for saving. For example, if saving takes the form of depreciable property used in a trade or business, depreciation deductions and the investment tax credit mitigate the additional income tax burden entailed in taxing both the amount saved and the subsequent income generated by the saving. But unless the present value of the depreciation deduction and investment credit equals the present value of the costs incurred to acquire the depreciable property—i.e., the amount saved, at least some of the additional cost of saving imposed by the income tax remains. To eliminate completely the extra tax on saving, the amount saved (equivalently, capital outlays) would have to be expensed—that is, deducted in full in the year in which the saving occurs—while the gross returns on the saving are included in taxable income as they are realized.

Apart from capital recovery deductions, a wide array of special provisions are generally noted as reducing the aggregate burden of the income taxes. These so-called "tax expenditures" are often characterized as subsidies, but are more appropriately to be seen as mitigations of the effects of the income tax in increasing the cost of saving and of effort relative to the cost of consumption and of leisure, respectively. Whatever case may be made for eliminating or reducing these "tax expenditures," doing so would raise the relative cost of effort and saving.

Price effects of government spending

It is frequently asserted that the real tax government imposes is to be found in its expenditures rather than in its tax levies *per se*. The reasoning is that these expenditures preempt the production resources of the nation for purposes determined in the political forum rather than in the marketplace, thereby depriving the private sector of these resources, the outputs they would produce, and the income claims generated by the production of these outputs. In a very broad sense, this view is correct: The resources transferred to government use and subject to its direction are not available for use as determined in the private sector. The pertinent question is how this preemption is effectuated. The answer to that question illustrates the nature of the impact of government spending on the economy.

---

many individuals the tax liability lies in the relatively remote future; the present value of the tax liability as it enters saving-consumption choices is relatively low except for the elderly or those contemplating inter-vivos transfers in the relatively near future. Notwithstanding, these taxes must be seen as incremental burdens on the returns to saving, hence as increasing the cost of saving relative to current consumption.

In the supply side analysis, the effects of government spending derive from the change in relative prices resulting from these outlays and the allocative responses to these price changes.

This proposition is most readily illustrated in the case of transfer payments to individuals. For example, unemployment compensation is usefully perceived as a negative tax on leisure, which reduces the cost of not working and raises the cost of employment. The response thereto is a shift in the use of the time and resources away from market-directed uses and toward leisure activities on the part of those persons for whom the unemployment compensation "hourly rate" more or less closely approximates the hourly pay rate net-of-taxes, and other costs of working (e.g., commuting costs, extra costs of meals, if any, etc.). Accordingly, unemployment compensation tends to accentuate reductions in employment during a business downturn and to inhibit employment gains after the cycle trough.

This conclusion contrasts sharply with the conventional notion that transfer payments of this sort tend to moderate the severity and shorten the duration of recessions. These favorable effects of such government outlays are based on the assumption that they augment aggregate demand, hence output and income, compared to the levels to which they would fall in the absence of these payments. But as shown earlier, while these payments may be effective in redistributing spending in the private sector, they cannot increase real total outlays. And by inhibiting renegotiation of wage rates and employment terms in order to make feasible the maintenance of employment levels, these transfer payments perversely accentuate the sharpness of decline and prolong recession.

This analysis applies, obviously, with respect to many transfer programs, including most of the payments under the welfare system. The effect of Medicaid in reducing the perceived cost of medical services to the beneficiaries, hence in increasing the amount of such services demanded at the real price of these services, has long been noted. Programs such as Aid for Families with Dependent Children obviously reduce the cost to the beneficiaries of being unemployed, as well as the cost of raising children.

Obviously, the supply side analysis of these government outlays does not address the humanitarian aspects of these programs. It does, however, explicate how these programs impact on the level and/or composition of economic activity. In particular, it shows that these programs should be seen as having none of the expansionary consequences attributed to them by the standard aggregate demand view of things. Indeed, the effects are to constrain the supplies of production inputs, particularly labor, to enhance downward rigidity of wage rates, and to distort relative prices of subsidized services.

These programs may nonetheless be deemed to be worthwhile; obviously they are since they continue to expand rather than to contract or disappear.

Government spending in the form of purchases of goods and services alters (explicit or implicit) relative prices by changing the composition of aggregate demand. Government purchases of any given product or service initially increases the demand for those products or services. This change in demand *per se* must increase the nominal price of the products or services, compared to the prices at which they would otherwise sell in the private sector. The consequence of this price distortion is a reduction in private sector purchases of these goods and services. The same sort of process, depending on the same kind of relative price changes, occurs in response to government purchases of production inputs, rather than products or services. In this case, the increase in demand occurs in the markets for the particular inputs, raising the market price faced by private sector purchasers of these inputs, hence reducing private sector purchases, thereby shifting their use from private sector to government sector outputs.

These changes in demand resulting from government purchases do not *per se* entail any change in the productivity of the production inputs involved. The real rate of return for any given quantity of any such input is, therefore, not altered. By the same token, the supply of the production inputs is not increased, although the allocation clearly is changed. No change in aggregate output, accordingly, results on this score from the government purchases.

The reallocation of production inputs, on the other hand, may result in a change in total real output if the real productivity of the inputs is enhanced or diminished in the government's, as opposed to the private sector's, use. A change in the amount of government purchases does not change total output and income by altering aggregate demand; any such change in real total income results only from changes in the effectiveness with which the production inputs are used. Changes in total output of this sort, obviously, need not be positively correlated with the amount of government purchases.

These relative price and allocative consequences of government spending are, clearly, of precisely the same character as those identified in the discussion of the price effects of taxation. It is in this sense that it is perfectly appropriate to delineate government spending as taxation. Identifying government outlays in this way, moreover, urges that their effects on the aggregate performance of the economy are of the same nature as those of taxation. This focus, clearly, is in sharp contrast with the conventional aggregate demand view which treats taxes as drains on aggregate income flows and government expenditures as additions thereto.

Price effects of monetary policy

In the supply side analysis, the analysis of the direct and initial effect of a change, particularly an unexpected change, in monetary aggregates focuses on the change in relative prices resulting therefrom. The basic assumption is that any such change disturbs portfolio equilibrium: the marginal utlity of the additional money falls below that of the other elements in the portfolio, impelling efforts to reduce the quantity of money and to increase the holdings of other goods and assets. This effort portends an increase in the level of prices at a rate greater than that anticipated prior to the (unexpected) acceleration of the monetary expansion.

The allocative response to the expected change in the future price level relative to the present resulting from changes in the pace of expansion of the money stock is, as one would expect, an opposite change in the allocation of current income between exercises of claims on output in the present vs. the future. A speedup of monetary expansion, implying an accelerating rate of gain in the price level in the future, induces an increase in the current demand for goods and services, at least for those which can be inventoried. This allocative effect, then, takes the form of increases in the proportion of current income used to purchase consumer durables and semidurables and a reduction in the portion of income that is saved.

The question is whether this unanticipated increase in nominal aggregate demand results as well in an increase in real output. If any such expansion of real output is to occur, there must be an increase in the amount of production inputs supplied. To obtain this result, one must either assume that suppliers of production inputs confuse increases in *nominal* for increases in *real* supply prices or that somehow the increase in the money stock reduces the cost of effort relative to leisure and/or the cost of saving and investing relative to consumption. But the increase in the money stock has no such relative price effect. Indeed, to the extent that it is identified as leading to an increase in the price level, it is far more likely to be seen as increasing the real cost of effort relative to leisure and of saving-investment relative to current consumption by way of its effects on real marginal tax rates. This perception, of course, would lead to a decrease in inputs supplied, hence to *cuts* in output.

These supply side hypotheses about the consequences of unexpected changes in the stock of money presuppose no significant institutional impediments to prompt changes of prices. In fact, various institutional factors are widely deemed to preclude prompt adjustment of contract terms and specific prices. The allocative adjustment, accordingly, may be impeded, taking the form of changes in the use of production inputs, hence in output, in response to the change in nominal aggregate demand. But notice that these real changes are functions of institutional rigidities and lead to temporary rather than long-term or permanent adjustments. Supply siders and monetarists are in perfect accord that in the long run, monetary magnitudes do not determine real output and income.

Supply side economic policies: dos and don'ts

The application of supply side analysis entails major changes in budgetary, fiscal, and monetary policies. A fundamental implication of the supply side analysis is that there is no pay-off in focusing fiscal policy on the control of aggregate demand. A corollary conclusion is that there is no valid purpose to be served by attempting to set government spending targets by reference to the supposed contribution of these outlays to aggregate demand. Similarly, a policy focus on the total amount of tax revenues is inappropriate as a means of influencing the level or change in total economic activity. In the same connection, the size of the deficit should not be perceived as a relevant variable for policy manipulation in the interests of attaining designated levels — or rates or growth in — employment, output, income, etc.

In denying the possibility of first-level income effects of fiscal actions, the supply side analysis also rejects the multiplier fiscal arithmetic as a basis for assessing the desirability of any given amount of taxes, government expenditures, or changes therein. Fiscal or budget policies predicated on the existence of a multiplicative relationship between changes in total taxes or total government outlay and total output and income are likely to fail of their explicit objectives — or succeed only by peradventure — and just as consequentially, are often likely to generate unintended and undesirable economic effects.

One of the major implications of these conclusions is that public economic policy should substantially forego short-run economic stabilization as a policy objective and focus, instead, on more attainable and more relevant concerns. These include reducing, if not eliminating, government-induced misallocation of the economy's production capacity resulting from the distortions of relative prices produced by taxation, spending, and regulatory policies. In consequence, the policy focus should shift to facilitating more efficient functioning of the private market system and to allowing the economy to achieve over the long run that rate of expansion of its total production potential and output which would result in the absence of existing constraints on supply.

Rejection of the aggregate demand approach in favor of the supply side analysis leads necessarily to a change in the appraisal of the effects of fiscal actions on the price level. In the aggregate demand analysis, tax and expenditure changes generate changes in aggregate demand which, since conditions of supply are deemed to be unchanged by fiscal actions, lead to increases or decreases in inflationary pressures. It is this point of view which leads those entertaining it to denounce tax reductions of the Kemp-Roth variety involving significant reductions in marginal tax rates as extraordinarily inflationary. In contrast, the supply side analysis delineates fiscal actions as impacting on aggregate demand in real terms only insofar as it first affects aggregate output by way of first-level price effects. Thus, an income tax rate reduction, by virtue of its relative price effects, generates increases in the supplies of labor and capital services and in output; increases in demand of equal magnitude are necessarily associated with the increase in output. In this analysis, accordingly, no increase in inflationary pressures results. Any such increase would have to be the consequence of an unnecessary increase in the rate of expansion of the stock of money. Indeed, if the growth in the stock of money were maintained at the same rate as if the tax rate reductions were not enacted, the increase in output resulting from the tax reduction would lead to a reduction in any upward pressure on the price level. It is this perception of how fiscal actions take effect that warrants characterizing Kemp-Roth as an anti-inflationary, supply side tax cut.

A collateral directive for tax policy strategy which comes from adopting the supply side analysis is to shift attention away from the level of tax liabilities in relation to income and toward marginal tax rates. In this connection, consider efforts to cancel or at least mitigate the effects of inflation on taxpayers' tax situations. In the past the standard response of the others opposing indexing of the tax system is that *effective* tax rates have been periodically reduced by discretionary tax changes, thereby cancelling the effects of inflation on real disposable income. Whether or not this is correct, it does not address the point which the supply side analysis identifies as at issue: that inflation raises the real *marginal* rates of tax and thereby discourages work and saving. The appropriate policy question is whether the discretionary tax changes of recent years have, in fact, cancelled the effects of inflation on real marginal tax rates.

Rigorous application of the supply side analysis leads to rejection of the view that budget deficits *per se* are inflationary or that increases in government outlays are the root cause of inflation. The pseudoscientific view of budget deficits as a source of inflation rests on the observation that those deficits tend to be monetized. This is not an inherent or necessary consequence of budget deficits. Much depends on how the deficit originates. Insofar as it results from tax or spending actions which depress or inadequately stimulate private-sector saving, and is financed by a greater monetary expansion than would otherwise occur, this in turn may result in accentuation of inflationary pressures (depending on what the thrust would have been absent the deficit). On the other hand, some fiscal actions, in particular supply side tax reductions which reduce the relative cost of saving, are likely to generate a sufficient increase in private sector saving to obviate the need for any monetary expansion to finance the deficit such tax cuts produce.

A major policy prescription which flows from this analysis is that the traditional institutional link between monetary expansion and government deficits should be broken. Monetary policy should take the form of slow and steady growth in the stock of money, substantially oblivious to budget prospects or outcomes.

Growth in government spending, even at very rapid rates, is not necessarily the cause of inflation. Government spending patterns, and the rate of spending expansion, are properly assessed in terms of their allocative effects and their consequent implications for the efficiency with which markets can operate. The tie between growth in spending and inflation is to be found in an excessively accomodating monetary policy. To repeat, this relationship should be terminated.

One of the principal analytical outputs of supply side economics is the rejection of the so-called "Phillips-curve" relationship between inflation and unemployment. By the same token, it rejects the view that price-level stability can be purchased only at the cost of unacceptably high levels of "unemployment" or that acceptable growth in employment depends on pursuit of fiscal and monetary policies likely to spur inflation.

On the contrary, the supply side analysis shows that public policy actions which are correctly designed to remove the impediments to employment and to saving and capital formation will constrain, not enhance, inflationary pressures. The root cause of inflation — increases in the overall level of prices — has always been too fast a growth in the stock of money relative to the growth in real output. It should be obvious that with any given rate of increase in the stock of money, the more effective tax measures are in increasing the supply of labor and in reducing tax bias against saving and investment, the less will be the upward pressure on the price level.

The corollary is that a monetary policy which succeeds in curbing inflation will enhance expansion of supplies of labor and capital services and total output and income. Inflation augments the existing tax bias against effort and saving by increasing the real marginal rates of income tax, thereby reducing the real after-tax returns for use of labor and capital services, hence constricting the expansion of labor and capital inputs and total output. Pursuit of a "tight" monetary policy, i.e., one which holds firmly to a steady, moderate rate of increase in the stock of money, accordingly, is not at odds with high rates of growth in output and employment. On the contrary, an antiinflationary monetary policy enhances the prospects for successful pursuit of those objectives.

Another major conclusion from the application of the supply side analysis of fiscal policy is that tax measures to promote higher rates of saving and capital formation are not at the expense of advancing the productivity and real wage rates of labor. On the contrary, effective implementation of these supply-side tax policies would enrich the capital:labor ratio, hence accelerate labor's productivity advance and increase the demand for and supply of labor services. Labor is likely to get some 75–80 percent of the gain in real GNP resulting from tax changes aimed at reducing constraints on saving and capital formation.

Conclusion

The intellectual origins of supply side economics are ancient, as the calendar of economics would date it, and are found in the works of Adam Smith, J. B. Say, and Alfred Marshall, to name only a few of the titans of the discipline. Its newness is to be found only in its applications to the public economic policy issues of contemporary American society. At this juncture, it affords a major addition to policy-makers' knowledge about how government actions interact with the economy. It offers great promise, therefore, for vastly improving public economic policies in the interests of more efficient functioning of the private market system, more rapid and solid growth in the stock of capital, steadier and stronger advances in labor's productivity, and more rapidly expanding total output and income.

THE THEORETICAL HERITAGE OF SUPPLY SIDE ECONOMICS

by

DAVID G. RABOY

David G. Raboy is Director of Research at the Institute for Research on the Economics of Taxation and former Associate Director of Tax Analysis at the National Association of Manufacturers.

BEFORE THE PASSAGE OF THE ECONOMIC RECOVERY TAX ACT of 1981, there was a great deal of handwringing in the press, in Congress, and among the experts over the efficacy of the policy precepts behind the "new" supply side economics. Critics argued that the policy proposals were too drastic because the theoretical underpinnings were untested. Once the tax act passed, a second wave of critics charged that supply side economics was the product of journalists and politicians, not economists, and that, in fact, there were no theoretical underpinnings.

Do supply side policies flow from logical, consistent, empirically verifiable economic theories or are they merely the whims of fanciful, fast-talking political operatives? In order to answer this question, one must decide just what brand of supply side economics one is considering. As is pointed out elsewhere in this volume, there is a wide spectrum of self-proclaimed supply side schools of thought. And, as is generally the case, the popular press has seized on the fringe ideas that stem from different sources to produce one giant, seemingly bizarre set of theories. If one derived all of one's information about supply side economics from the popular press and made a kind of composite supply sider, one would have to conclude that a supply sider categorically rejects monetarism and considers Milton Friedman to be the most dangerous heretic since Keynes; believes not only that tax cuts are self-financing, but that the cutting of taxes can cure any economic ill; and, most astonishing of all, that taxes can explain any event from the Great Depression to Third World Revolution.

Nothing quite as exotic as all that will be used to define supply side economics here. In fact, this body of thought, as defined here, is surprisingly mainstream, having as its forbears the men from earlier times who first described the free market system. To consider oneself a supply side economist, one only has to agree with most of the following empirical and theoretical statements:

1. The market system provides the most efficient vehicle for the allocation of resources.

2. The market is a stable mechanism because the forces of supply and demand guarantee that markets clear.

3. The market adjusts to price changes relatively quickly.

4. Explicitly incorporating information costs in the market mechanism, it is recognized that the economy is more or less in continuous equilibrium.

5. Individuals and firms are rational and engage in normal optimizing behavior.

Add to these some beliefs about the responsiveness of investors and workers to after-tax rewards, and you have a supply side economist. It should be clear from all this that the terms neoclassical and supply side are synonymous, and thus the heritage of supply side economics is the heritage of modern neoclassical theory.

The purpose of this essay is to trace the development of free-market economics from early times to the present. The obvious conclusion is that today's supply side theory is the culmination of over two-hundred years of an evolutionary process, beginning with Adam Smith and J. B. Say, continuing through the marginalist revolution and the birth of neoclassicalism, embodied in the works of Alfred Marshall as well as the writings of A. C. Pigou and Vilfredo Pareto. In modern times the process has been furthered by such men as Arnold Harberger, Milton Friedman, and Martin Feldstein, as well as by the multitude of young writers who have contributed to the "optimal taxation" and "public choice" literature, such as Michael Boskin.

Adam Smith

No discussion of free market economics would be complete without a review of the teachings of Adam Smith. Although he wrote long before the application of rigorous mathematical methods to economic concepts, his teachings established, heuristically, the basis for much of what was to follow concerning the efficient functioning of an economy. Smith, who lived from 1723 to 1790, was influenced by the great "natural law" philosophers of his day. His major contribution to economic thought, *An Inquiry into the Nature and Causes of the Wealth of Nations*, twelve years in the making, was published in 1776.

The Wealth of Nations was a response to mercantilism, then the economic theory in England. Proponents of the mercantile view believed that the mother country was supreme and that government should play an activist role in trade. They advocated protective tariffs, the establishment of monopoly trading companies, and other protectionist schemes as the best way to insure a healthy domestic economy.

Smith countered that, in fact, an economy could only reach its pinnacle in the presence of two ingredients—unbridled expression of individual self-interest, and the existence of an unencumbered free market system. Smith's argument was not just that individual satisfaction could be maximized in this manner, but that the welfare of society as a whole would be, too.

Although primarily a response to mercantilism, Smith's arguments have become the basis of many economic models in many different areas, from theories of the benefits of international trade to the specification of an efficient tax system in the realm of Public Finance Economics. In fact, these seminal thoughts became the basis for the unified theory of overall societal welfare developed by later neoclassicists.

For the moment, taking the existence of a free market as a given, it is individual self-interest that dictates the ebb and flow of economic activity:

> Give me that which I want, and ye shall have this that you want...it is in this manner that we obtain from one another the far greater part of those good offices which we stand in need of. It is not from the benevolence of the butcher, the brewer, or the baker that we expect our dinner, but from their regard to their own self interest.[1]

The prevailing theories of the period stressed the benevolence of an activist government or, at least, the benevolence of powerful members of society as necessary for the economic well being of a nation. Smith disagreed. Clearly, individuals will seek that which they desire. Since some individuals may possess more or less of a given commodity than they desire relative to some other commodity, individual satisfaction can be improved through exchange. This holds true for any economic entity — a physical product, labor, or even the exchange of command over goods now for command over goods in the future. Thus, free trade, involving either one's labor or on the international scene, translates wants and desires into economic growth and the highest level of societal welfare. Such growth, a result of the division of labor:

> ...from which so many advantages are derived, is not originally the effect of any human wisdom, which forsees and intends that general opulence to which it gives occasion. It is the necessary, though very slow and gradual consequence of a certain propensity in human nature which has in view no such extensive utility; the propensity to truck, barter, and exchange one thing for another.[2]

As an example, consider the case of Roberts and Jones. Roberts springs full blown into this world with an endowment of a thousand

---

[1] Adam Smith, *The Wealth of Nations*, (London: J.M. Dent and Sons, Ltd. 1937), p. 13.
[2] *Ibid.*, p. 12.

pancakes, while Jones is bequeathed several cases of maple syrup. Now Roberts could attempt to eek out his life forcing wads of dry pancakes down his throat while Jones quafs endless snifters of gooey syrup. Each, in his own meager way, would survive and reach some level of well being. But they would be much better off if they bartered pancakes and syrup. The overall level of satisfaction of each is improved simply due to the reallocation of resources affected by unencumbered trade. In a diverse economy with a multitude of products, including the services of labor, ratios of exchange can be set up through this trading mechanism until everyone is more satisfied than they were with their initial endowment alone.

This theme dominated the writings of classical economists; if only exchange were free, then people would be free to sell their labor in an optimal manner, and the economy could operate efficiently. Of course, this view was predicated on the belief that not only was free exchange possible, but the market is inherently stable. Trade and self interest would be ineffectual if the economy oscillated widely, never reaching an equilibrium of supply and demand. Thus, a second condition for economic efficiency is that markets clear. Adam Smith was confident that this would happen at what he called the "natural price" of a commodity. No other price could exist for very long because the natural forces of supply and demand would operate until the natural price was reached:

> When the quantity brought to market falls short of the effectual demand, all those who are willing to pay...cannot be supplied with the quantity they want. Rather than want it altogether, some of them will be willing to give more...
>
> When the quantity brought to market exceeds the effectual demand, it cannot be sold to those who are willing to pay...in order to bring it thither. Some part must be sold to those who are willing to pay less, and the low price which they get for it must reduce the price of the whole...
>
> When the quantity brought to market is just sufficient to supply the effectual demand, and not more, the market price naturally comes to be...the same with the natural price. The whole quantity upon hand can be disposed of for this price, and cannot be disposed of for more. The competition of the different dealers obliges them all to accept of this price, but does not oblige them to accept of less.[3]

Thus, it is competition that guarantees the stability of the economy, according to Smith. With individuals following their own self-interest, competition insures an equilibrium because, for instance,

---

[3]*Ibid.*, pp. 49–50.

should a price be higher than warranted, someone would make a profit by undercutting it.

A corollary, then, involves the role of government and the effects of government actions on the expression of self-interest and competition. Far from increasing commerce, in Smith's view, controls and subsidies had distorted the allocation of resources, resulting in a net loss to society. Government intervention, monopoly, or other interferences with the free flow of market information could only work to the detriment of society. Having rejected benevolence as a necessary condition for the betterment of society, Smith believed that the benefits of trade, competition, and self-interest would permeate all sectors of society with the result that "a general quantity diffuses itself to all the different ranks of society."[4]

To Smith, the general morality of a nation and individual self-interest, far from being incompatible, were complementary. Smith was very concerned in his writing with less fortunate social classes, and considered the betterment of such classes a priority.

> Is this improvement in the circumstance, of the people to be regarded as an advantage or an inconvenience to the society? The answer seems at first sight abundantly plain. Servants, labourers, and workmen of different kinds, make up the greater part of every great political society. But what improves the circumstances of the greater part can never be regarded as an inconveniency to the whole. No society can surely be flourishing and happy, of which the far greater part of the members are poor and miserable. It is but equity, besides, that they who feed, clothe, and lodge the whole body of people, would have a share of the produce of their own labour as to be themselves tolerably well fed, clothed, and lodged.[5]

The existence of "perfect liberty," which Smith held so important, would then result in the development of the two key ingredients which would guarantee "that universal opulence which extends itself to the lowest ranks of people."[6]

Actually, these two ingredients are interrelated. The first is widespread division of labor which Smith believed resulted in "the greatest improvement in the productive powers of labour."[7] But the division of labor cannot occur in the absence of a steady rate of growth in the accumulation of physical capital. Capital was viewed as the key to labor productivity in that "labour is facilitated and abridged by the application of proper machinery."[8] Thus, it is in the entrepreneur's

---

[4]*Ibid.*, p. 10.
[5]*Ibid.*, p. 70.
[6]*Ibid.*, p. 10.
[7]*Ibid.*, p. 4.
[8]*Ibid.*, p. 9.

interest to invest. But laborers, too, have an interest in investment, according to Smith, because the demand for labor varies directly with the rate of capital accumulation:

> The demand for those who live by wages... necessarily increases with the increase of the revenue and stock of every country, and cannot possibly increase without it.[9]

Capital accumulation represented increases in wealth to Smith and was crucial to productivity, employment, division of labor, and thus, to the betterment of the lower classes. Economic growth itself was inextricably linked to the rate at which the capital stock expanded. Because this variable was so crucial to Adam Smith, a great deal of his writing concerned the determinants of a healthy rate of capital formation in the economy.

Capital accumulation, of course, is impossible without saving. To Smith, a high rate of economic growth was dependent on modest consumption and a healthy rate of savings. The Keynesians would later turn this theory on its head, but it is interesting to note that this debate occurred even in Smith's day. Of course, in the Keynesian view, consumption leads to increases in aggregate demand, which leads to increases in investment via the accelerator principle. Implicit in Smith's writing is the idea that saving is the driving force behind investment in that "whatever industry might acquire, if parsimony did not save and store up, the capital would never be the greater."[10]

Smith stressed this again and again in his writings. And latter-day economists have often echoed Smith's observation that the process of capital accumulation is merely the process of deferring consumption from one period to another. Whatever a person does not consume, he adds to his "capital." If everyone saves, the stock of capital will increase for the entire economy. Saving is the key because, "Capitals are increased by parsimony, and diminished by prodigality and misconduct."[11]

It is the lack of saving that is responsible for economic problems, according to Smith, not a lack of the desire to consume:

> The proportion between capital and revenue, therefore, seems everywhere to regulate the proportion between industry and idleness. Wherever capital predominates, industry prevails: wherever reve-

---
[9]*Ibid.*, p. 61.
[10]*Ibid.*, p. 301.
[11]*Ibid.*, p. 301.

nue, idleness. Every increase or diminution of capital, therefore, naturally tends to increase or diminish the real quantity of industry, the number of productive hands, and consequently, the exchangeable value of the annual produce of the land and labour of the country, the real wealth and revenue of all its inhabitants.[12]

In the period following World War II, when the Keynesian-neoclassical synthesis was taking shape, much was written about the relationship between the rate of profit and the wage rate, and their relationship to the rate of investment. The "neoclassical parables" stated that as the capital stock expanded, the rate of profit would fall and the real wage rate would increase. The explanation for this will become clear when other latter-day economists are discussed, but it is interesting to note that Adam Smith also argued along these lines. In Smith's view, workers had a vested interest in a high savings rate because this would lead to increased capital formation and higher real wages. Profit, however, was not a dirty word because, given the risks inherent in investment, a healthy profit rate was necessary to induce investment, in the absence of which labor would stagnate.

The debate over the role of government is the same today as it was in the time of Adam Smith. Economists continue to argue the pros and cons of self-interest, to fight over the stability of the market, and to stress saving over consumption or vice versa. Of course, the mode of analysis of classical economists such as Smith involved intuition as opposed to rigorous application of mathematical logic. Yet, it is of more than passing interest that Smith's intuition was fully supported by the work of later neoclassicists.

Of course, the writings of Adam Smith have not been taken seriously by most contemporary policy makers in the United States. But this is not cause to worry, if one accepts Smith's optimism, because individuals will prosper despite the meddling of government:

> This frugality and good conduct, however, is upon most occasions, it appears from experience, sufficient to compensate, not only the private prodigality and misconduct of individuals, but the public extravagance of government. The uniform, constant, and uninterrupted effort of every man to better his condition, the principle from which public and national, as well as private, opulence is originally derived, is frequently powerful enough to maintain the natural progress of things towards improvement, in spite both of the extravagance of government and the greatest errors of administration. Like the unknown principle of animal life, it frequently restores health and

---

[12]*Ibid.*

vigor to the constitution, in spite, not only of the disease, but of the absurd prescriptions of the doctor.[13]

This, some would argue, explains the amazing resiliency of the American economy despite the "extravagance of government."

Jean Baptiste Say

The job of systematizing Adam Smith's concepts fell to a man who was only nine years old when *Wealth of Nations* was first published. That man was Jean Baptiste Say, who lived from 1767 to 1832, and founded the French classical school of economics. Say's most famous work was *A Treatise on Political Economy*, which was published in 1803 and was much in demand in the United States during the first half of the nineteenth century.[14]

One of the most misunderstood and misquoted concepts in the history of economic thought has become known as Say's Law. The popular perception of Say's Law is actually John Maynard Keynes' interpretation of Say's writing. Thus, Say's Law has become known as the proposition that "supply creates its own demand," and the corollary, that there cannot be any overproduction of any single good. "Post-Keynesian"[15] writers echoed Keynes' interpretation. For instance, Luigi Pasinetti once wrote that Say "stated that any production generates *its own* demand" (my emphasis) defining "what has then become universally known as *la loi des debouches* or 'Say's Law.' "[16] Statements like this misrepresent the contribution of J. B. Say.

As a backdrop to Say's writing, consider a conflict, important in Say's period, that would become dormant for a long time, only to flare up in Keynes' day and continue to this day. On one side of the conflict was Robert Malthus, who argued that Adam Smith's belief that competition would automatically guarantee economic welfare and full employment was wrong.[17] In a long running debate with the classical economist David Ricardo, Malthus, responding to the writings of Say and John Stuart Mill, questioned the desirability of industrial expansion and argued that unrestrained investment would lead to overproduction and economic stagnation;[18] this distrust of saving and investment was later embodied in the "paradox of thrift" beliefs of Keynes. Indeed, Keynes traces theories of "effective de-

---

[13]*Ibid.*, p. 306.
[14]Charles W. Needy, *Classics of Economics*, (Moore Publishing Company, Inc. 1980), p. 18.
[15]"Post-Keynesian" is the label attached to supporters of Keynes opposed to neoclassical analysis, who wrote in the post-World War II period. Included are Joan Robinson, Luigi Pasinetti, and Nicholas Kaldor.
[16]Luigi L. Pasinetti, *Growth and Income Distribution*, (Cambridge University Press, 1974), p. 30.
[17]Everett Burtt, Jr., *Social Perspectives in the History of Economic Theory* (New York: St. Martin's Press 1972) p. 89.
[18]*Ibid.*

mand" to Malthus. In retrospect, post-Keynesians have also cited the views of Malthus as seminal:

> Among the views that Malthus attacked was the traditional one that 'every frugal man is a public benefactor.' He retorted that 'the principle of saving, pushed to excess, would destroy the motive of production.' And he added that 'if production is in great excess above consumption, the motive to accumulate and produce must cease from the want of will to consume.' On this basis, Malthus defended the unproductive consumption of the landlords as remedy to 'market gluts,' and warned against the dire consequences of 'parsimony and thrift.'[19]

Thus, in direct response to Say's law, what was to become the Keynesian theory of effective demand found its roots, and a classic confrontation over the efficacy of saving versus consuming began. But before turning to Say's concepts, a digression on "effective demand" is necessary.

The basic principle of "effective demand" goes something like this: In a modern industrial society, the actual productive potential of an economy may exceed actual demand, leading to under-utilization of resources, unemployment, and economic stagnation. In this view, the government should intervene to stimulate consumption and thus bring the level of effective demand up to the level of productive potential. This view is predicated on the belief that overall gluts can occur for significant periods in an economy.

Say did not believe that general gluts could occur, nor did he believe in the efficacy of government-stimulated consumption:

> It is common to hear adventurers in the different channels of industry assert, that their difficulty lies not in the production, but in the disposal of commodities; that products would always be abundant, if there were but a ready demand, or market for them...But ask them what peculiar causes and circumstances facilitate the demand for their products, and you will soon perceive that most of them have extremely vague notions of these matters;...that they treat doubtful points as matters of certainty, often pray for what is directly opposite their interests, and importunately solicit from authority a protection of the most devious tendency.[20]

In Say's view, demand was not constrained by the desire to consume, but rather by the level of wealth or production in society. In modern microeconomic theory, economists explain this as a lack of "absolute satiation." Theoretically, there may be some point where individuals have consumed so much that they have no desire to con-

---

[19]Luigi L. Pasinetti, op. cit., pp. 29–30.
[20]J. B. Say, *A Treatise on Political Economy*, (New York: Augustus M. Kelly, 1964), p. 132.

sume further. But any realistic observer of the world will immediately realize that society is nowhere near the point of absolute satiation, has never been there in the past, and is not likely to reach that point in the forseeable future. In fact, wants and desires can be said to be unlimited. Then it becomes clear that consumption is limited not because of any lack of desire to consume, but rather because of a lack of means. This was Say's contribution:

> A man who applies his labour to the investing of objects with value by the creation of utility of some sort, can not expect such a value to be appreciated and paid for, unless where other men have the means of purchasing it. Now, of what do these means consist? Of other values of other products, likewise the fruits of industry, capital, and land. Which leads us to a conclusion that may at first sight appear paradoxical, namely, that it is production which opens a demand for products.[21]

Say's law of markets does not claim that a supply of a specific good creates a demand for that specific good, but rather that the overall level of demand in the economy is dependent on the level of output, and that as production and capital accumulation accelerate, so will demand.

The second challenge facing Say was the flip side of the previous argument: the belief that investment would lead to overproduction and economic stagnation. Say, antedating the neoclassical tradition, believed that, due to the interworkings of supply and demand in the marketplace, prices were flexible. An excess of any particular item could exist at a specific point in time, but no general glut in the economy could exist. Say also argued that the glut of a particular good is caused "either because it has been produced in excessive abundance, or because production of other commodities has fallen short."[22] This latter cause is restated as "people have bought less because they have made less profit."[23] Say noted that a glut of one commodity is paralleled by an identical scarcity of another. Such scarcities, he believed, indicate that consumers prefer the scarce commodity. If the market is allowed to function, resources will naturally flow in the direction of the preferred activity, eliminating both glut and scarcity. It is when the market is interfered with that disequilibrium is maintained:

> It is observable, moreover, that precisely at the same time that one commodity makes a loss, another commodity is making an excessive profit. And, since such profits must operate as a powerful stimulus to

---
[21] *Ibid.*, p. 133.
[22] *Ibid.*, p. 135.
[23] *Ibid.*

the cultivation of that particular kind of product, there must needs be some violent means, or some extraordinary cause, a political or natural convulsion, or the avarice or ignorance of authority, to perpetuate this scarcity on the one hand, and consequent glut on the other. No sooner is the cause of this political disease removed, than the means of production feel a natural impulse towards the vacant channels, the replenishment of which restores activity to all the others. One kind of production would seldom outstrip every other, and its products be disproportionately cheapened, were production left entirely free.[24]

At the close of Say's chapter "Of the Demand or Market for Products" in his *Treatise on Political Economy*, four conclusions are offered. The first is that in any area profits will rise "the more numerous are the producers, and the more various their production,"[25] as well as the more extensive the markets. Thus, there is agreement between Say and Adam Smith on the relationship between competition and prosperity. In his second conclusion, Say reiterates that "the success of one branch of industry promotes that of all others,"[26] and in the third, he quarrels with those that would interfere with the normal flow of international trade. In his fourth conclusion, J. B. Say argues that the unnatural encouragement of consumption "is no benefit to commerce,"[27] and states that "it is the goal of good government to stimulate production, of bad to encourage consumption."[28]

Say also attempted to eliminate the confusion surrounding the role of money in society. The concept of "the neutrality of money," or whether or not money affects real values in the economy, has been a source of debate throughout the history of economic thought. In Say's time, insufficient demand was often blamed on a shortage of money. But to Say, "sales cannot be dull because money is scarce, but because other products are so."[29] Money, in Say's view, was nothing mystical and merely "performs but a momentary function in this double exchange; and when the transaction is finally closed, it will always be found, that one kind of commodity has been exchanged for another."[30]

Once again, Say echoed Smith's view that a free, competitive society would allocate resources to their most efficient uses. The analysis held that "the natural wants of society" would lead to relatively higher demand for preferred products and that in these indus-

---
[24] *Ibid.*
[25] *Ibid.*, p. 137.
[26] *Ibid.*
[27] *Ibid.*, p. 139.
[28] *Ibid.*
[29] *Ibid.*, p. 134.
[30] *Ibid.*

tries "productive services are somewhat better paid than in the rest."[31] Higher profits would attract additional producers "and thus the nature of the products is always regulated by the wants of society."[32] This concept would become the cornerstone of the unified theory of the neoclassical school: All activities in the economy flow from the domain of "consumer sovereignty"; that is, investment, production, and all other activities in the society could be traced to the sum of the rational, subjective wants and desires of the populace.

J. B. Say also had a thing or two to say about taxes, and was rather opinionated on the subject. He stated that "[i]t is a glaring absurdity to pretend that taxation contributes to national wealth ...Indeed, it would be trifling with my reader's time, did not most governments act upon this principle."[33] As early as 1803, Say rejected the ancester of a backward bending labor supply curve by refusing to accept "that the pressure of taxation impels the productive classes to redouble their exertions."[34] He argued that taxation retarded capital formation because "capital is but an accumulation of the very products that taxation takes from the subject."[35] Capital, he believed, was the key to increases in the nation's wealth, and, as others still argue today, suggested that taxes should be levied "[s]uch as are least injurious to reproduction."[36]

The Marginalists

The work of Adam Smith and J. B. Say went a long way in describing the conditions under which an economy would thrive and reach its productive potential. But much of the argument rested purely on intuitive reasoning and many analytical questions remained unanswered. Just what was it that guaranteed maximum well-being under a system of "perfect liberty"? Could it be proven in a logical, rigorous fashion that the forces of competition and self interest moved the economy, via the "invisible hand," towards the production of output with the highest value to society? And, by the way, just what is this thing called value?

A hallmark of supply side economics is the assertion that economic decision making occurs at the margin: A worker determines how much he will work after observing the after-tax wage rate on additional hours of work, not by referring back to hours already worked. With that information, he will decide whether to spend his extra

---

[31] *Ibid.*, p. 143.
[32] *Ibid.*, p. 144.
[33] *Ibid.*, p. 447.
[34] *Ibid.*
[35] *Ibid.*
[36] *Ibid.*, p. 449.

hours at work or at leisure. It is, as stated earlier in this volume, the relative costs facing economic actors that determines their behavior, and in a broader sense, the way in which scarce resources are distributed in society.

In the mid-nineteenth century, a group of economists that was to become known as the "marginalists" advanced economic theory a great deal with their theories of value and resource allocation. Indeed, marginalist theory, involving concepts of relative scarcity and prices, is the basis for modern microeconomic theory. Simultaneously, but independently, three economists developed theories explaining the determination of prices and economic value. These three were Carl Menger, William Stanley Jevons and Leon Walras.

Carl Menger (1840 to 1921) received his education in Krakow, Poland, and was credited with being the leader of the so-called Austrian school. His two most famous works were *Principles of Economics*, published in 1871, and *Problems of Economics and Sociology*, published in 1883. Jevons (1835 to 1882) was born in Liverpool, England and educated in London. Leon Walras (1839 to 1910), who was largely self-taught, was born in France, but taught at the Academy of Lausanne in Switzerland. In addition to these three, important contributions were made by others on both sides of the Atlantic. Antoine-Augustin Cournot was one of the first to mathematize economic concepts. Frederick von Weisser, a student of Mengers, would actually coin the phrase, "marginal utility," so familiar to students of microeconomic theory. The United States was not entirely absent from the marginalist revolution. John Bates Clark (1847 to 1938), educated at Brown University and Amherst college, also made important additions to economic theory.[37]

During the development of early classical economics, one of the big topics of debate concerned determination of economic value. Just how might an economist decide what contributed to the value of a commodity and what didn't? This, of course, was crucial because such a determination was a prerequisite to the determination of the types of systems and government activities that would lead to a maximization of economic value. Adam Smith and David Ricardo argued that the amount of labor used in the production of a commodity determined the value. Say quarrelled with this "labor theory of value," and pointed out that the prices of certain goods did not reflect their labor content. Instead, he believed that value depended on something he called "utility," but his definition was too loose to be satisfying.

That the classical theories of value, both utility and labor, were in-

---

[37]Charles W. Needy, op. cit., pp. 109–112.

sufficient was illustrated by what was known as the "water-diamond paradox." Water, though essential to human life, was considered to be much less valuable than, say, diamonds. This caused considerable consternation among economic thinkers, who were hard pressed to explain the paradox scientifically. In the writings of the marginalists, the explanation became apparent.

In Carl Menger's view, what was lacking in economic theory was a unified explanation of value. Economic theory, according to Menger, should be totally divorced from subjectivity. Instead, he felt that economics must assume the characteristics of "pure" sciences like chemistry, biology, or physics.[38] Thereafter, economic concepts should be "positive" rather than "normative."

Menger's jumping off point was his belief that all value could be traced back to the individual wants and desires of the citizenry. In the later, neoclassical period, this would be known as the belief in "consumer sovereignty."

Given individual wants, what determined which goods would be produced? Menger set four criteria: There had to be a human need for the good in question, there had to be the physical possibility of fulfilling that need, humans had to be cognizant of the source of satisfaction, and they had to have the power to direct the knowledge.[39]

But how did individual wants and desires translate into the allocation of resources and the value of that allocation? Menger observed that within a given period, the consumption of successive units of goods provided different degrees of satisfaction. As more units are consumed, the pleasure associated with each additional unit declines. At some point, additional consumption provides no satisfaction whatsoever. Menger coupled this observation with the dilemma of an individual who desires to reach the highest level of satisfaction possible with limited means.[40] The calculus analogue to this problem is the classic case of constrained optimization. In pragmatic terms, identical problems confront an individual wishing to allocate his scarce time between work and leisure or to allocate his limited resources between saving and consumption in order that he may reach his highest level of satisfaction.

Assume that two goods yield the same price in the market, and that an individual has fully exhausted his income purchasing quantities of the two goods. If the utility derived from the last unit of good X is greater than that of good Y, the individual has not maximized his satisfaction. At the same price, given the same resources, the

---

[38]Everett Burtt, Jr., op. cit., p. 182.
[39]*Ibid.*, p. 184.
[40]*Ibid.*, p. 185.

consumer can purchase X instead of Y and increase his enjoyment more. Further, as X is substituted for Y, the additional satisfaction gained from each additional purchase of X decreases. In fact, the sensible consumer will adjust his purchases to the point where, if both goods cost the same, the satisfaction from consumption of an additional unit of each good will be exactly the same. This result was intuitively obvious to Menger although he never used the phrase "marginal utility" (which refers to the additional satisfaction from consuming an additional unit).

It is the principle of marginal utility that leads to the free trade or exchange that was so important to Adam Smith. Consider the case where an individual is given an original endowment of two goods, the combination of which might not produce the highest possible level of satisfaction. Another individual may be endowed with a mix of goods that is also suboptimal—different people will value goods differently, and it is possible that marginal utilities for different goods, at some level, will vary across individuals. If the utility I assign a unit of good X is more than what I assign good Y, but you value Y more highly, the basis for a trade exists. I will be willing to give you units of Y in return for units of X. Remember that as a person consumes more of a good, additional units become less valuable. Thus, trading will continue until the marginal value we have placed on X just equals Y. At this point, both you and I will have reached the highest level of satisfaction possible given our original endowments.

This idea can be applied to any goods or services in the economy including capital, labor, leisure, or other items. If the means to exchange are unencumbered, individuals can trade commodities of low subjective utility for those that are high, and individuals can better themselves as a result. This concept provides the basis for later theories of economic efficiency.

At this point the water-diamond paradox is resolved. The relative values of goods are determined by their relative scarcities. The reason that water is valued less than diamonds is that it is much more abundant. In general, all our needs for water can be satisfied, while our desire for diamonds cannot; that is, the marginal utility from a "unit" of diamonds is much higher than that for water. We value them much more. Of course, on a desert, the valuation of diamonds relative to water may be considerably different—the last unit of water may be worth a thousand diamonds.

Menger's analysis provides a crucial building block for supply side economics. Economic choices are made on the basis of the value of incremental or marginal units—economic decision making occurs at the margin. Then the way in which taxes, monetary theory, or government spending will affect economic behavior depends on their effects at the margin, on the valuation of activities or commodities.

Another major contribution came from William Stanley Jevons, who further explained the concepts of marginal utility and the role of prices in allocating resources. Jevons stressed, as did Menger, that satisfaction would decrease as additional units of a good were consumed. In Jevon's terminology, marginal utility was the "variation of the final degree of utility."[41]

Utility, in Jevons view, could be either positive or negative; that is, concepts of marginal utility could be extended to things that were painful or involved exertion, such as work. Jevons came to the same conclusion as Menger, that distribution would cease when the additional satisfaction derived from one commodity equaled that of another.

Most important to an understanding of supply side economics, however, is Jevon's work concerning prices. He made the point, stressed earlier in this volume, that resource allocation is affected by changing relative prices. As the first building block, Jevons pointed out that in competitive markets, at any point in time, uniform goods must have exactly the same price:

> If, in selling a quantity of perfectly equal and uniform barrels of flour, a merchant arbitrarily fixes different prices on them, a purchaser would of course select the cheaper ones; and where there was absolutely no difference in the thing purchased, even an excess of a penny in the price of a thing worth a thousand pounds, would be a valid ground of choice. Hence follows what is undoubtedly true, with proper explanations, that in the same open market, at any one moment, there cannot be two prices for the same kind of article. Such differences as may practically occur arise from extraneous circumstances, such as the defective credit of purchasers, their imperfect knowledge of the market, and so on.[42]

This has been called the "Law of Indifference" and, in tandem with other concepts of marginalism, it leads to a very powerful theory of value and exchange. One more ingredient is necessary, the determination of the market price of a good. Jevons has the answer:

> Thus, from the self-evident principle, stated earlier, that there cannot, in the same market, at the same moment, be two different prices for the same uniform commodity, it follows that the last increments in

---

[41] William Stanley Jevons, "The Theory of Political Economy," in Charles W. Needy, op. cit., p. 118.
[42] *Ibid.*, p. 126.

an active exchange must be exchanged in the same ratio as the whole quantity exchanged.[43]

If, in a competitive economy, a commodity can command only one price, then it is obvious that that price represents the cost of additional consumption to the individual. A rational individual will make purchases up to the point where the additional cost is just justified by the additional benefit of consumption. If the benefit were higher, it would behoove the individual to consume more, but if the cost exceeded the benefit, the consumer would be happier if he decreased his purchases. Jevons illustrated one of the cornerstones of modern microeconomic theory—that an individual will consume up to the point where the price of an additional unit just equals its marginal utility.

If this is true for one good, it is true for all. If I apply this rule for goods X and Y, then it is obvious that the ratio of the marginal utilities of these two goods will equal the ratio of their prices, or in Jevon's words:

> The keystone of the whole theory of Exchange, and of the principal problems of economics lies in this proposition—the ratio of exchange of any two commodities will be the reciprocal of the ratio of the final degrees of utility of the quantities of commodity available for consumption after the exchange is completed.[44]

Jevon's idea is crucial to supply side theory, which also stresses the importance of relative prices. Should the price of one thing change in relation to another, economic behavior will change. If the price of X increases relative to Y, people will buy relatively more of Y. This is because, after the price increase, the cost of consuming X exceeds the benefit. People reduce their consumption of X until the satisfaction gained from the last unit has risen to the new price of X. As an example, should the cost of working increase (relative to not working) due to a tax increase, individuals will increase their leisure time until equilibrium is restored. Jevon's work was crucial because by analyzing the interrelationship of utility, scarcity, and prices, he provided strong ammunition to combat the classical labor theory of value. His unified theory resolved another paradox:

> The mere fact that there are many things, such as rare, ancient books, coins, antiquities, and etc., which have high value, and which are absolutely incapable of production now, dispenses the notion that

---
[43] *Ibid.*
[44] *Ibid.*, pp. 127–28.

value depends on labour. Even those things which are producible in any quantity by labour seldom exchange exactly at the corresponding value.[45]

The unified theory can explain all value, not just that of manufactured goods. But Jevons also pointed out that while labor did not determine value, it contributed to it via the production process. The amount of labor input affected the supply of output which in turn affected scarcity and thus marginal utility.[46]

One final contribution by Jevons is notable, and that concerns the valuation of factors of production. Jevons turned the classical notion that labour determines value on its head to point out that it is the value of output that determines the value of labor. Jevons held labor to be "essentially variable, so that its value must be determined by the value of produce, not the value of produce by that of labour."[47] This concept, that the productivity of labor determines its real wage rate, is also part of the supply side view.

The relationship between value, marginal benefit, and prices has been discussed above. Leon Walras examined how these forces interact in the aggregate to produce an equilibrium yielding the highest level of social welfare possible. Today, he is viewed as the father of "general equilibrium" economics. Walras coined the term "rarete" to represent the satisfaction derived from the consumption of an additional unit. With Jevons, Walras concluded that "current prices or equilibrium prices are equal to the ratios of the raretes."[48] Implicit is the assumption that trade or exchange is unencumbered, in which case "[v]alue and exchange...arises spontaneously in the market as the result of the competition."[49] Walras, like the neoclassicists after him, believed that economic efficiency could only result from the free market:

> The exchange of two commodities for each other in a perfectly competitive market is an operation by which all holders of either one, or of both, of the two commodities can obtain the greatest possible satisfaction of their wants consistent with the condition that the two commodities are bought and sold at one and the same rate of exchange throughout the market.[50]

Finally, we must consider the contribution of the American J. B. Clark to the marginalist revolution. The concepts reviewed here in-

---

[45]*Ibid.*, p. 130.
[46]*Ibid.*
[47]*Ibid.*
[48]Leon Walras, "Elements of Pure Economics," in Charles W. Needy, op cit., p. 143.
[49]*Ibid.*
[50]*Ibid.*, p. 142.

volve an extension of the marginal utility concept to the theory of the demand for labor and the determination of wages. Clark applied the concepts to a slightly different question. The output produced by adding an additional worker, if all else is held constant, is referred to in today's jargon as the "marginal product of labor." Clark discussed what is now referred to as the "diminishing marginal productivity of labor." In basic terms, given a fixed supply of capital, as additional workers are applied to this stock of capital, total output will increase, but at a decreasing rate.

For example, if ten workers and five machines produce one hundred widgets, eleven workers and five machines produce one hundred and twenty, and twelve workers with the same machines produce one hundred and thirty, a pattern is identified. Adding an eleventh worker increased output by twenty (the marginal product of the eleventh worker is twenty) but adding a twelfth worker increased output by only ten units. The marginal product has decreased from twenty to ten; hence the phenomenon of diminishing marginal productivity. Clark's view was that the value of all labor was dependent on the value of the marginal unit:

> The effective value of any unit of labor is always what the whole society, with all its capital, produces minus what it would produce if the unit were taken away. This sets the universal standard of pay.[51]

This was Clark's law of wages which stated that "[e]ach unit of labor, then, is worth to its employer what the last unit produces."[52]

That labor will receive such a wage is guaranteed if competition among employers is present. A relevant unit of labor "has in its hands a certain potential product, when it offers its services to employers. If one set of entrepreneurs will not give them the value of it, another one will, provided that competition is perfect."[53] Thus, wages are dependent on labor productivity.

The unified theory of value, and the relevance of comparing costs and benefits in economic decisionmaking, was summed up by Frederick von Weisser, who was a student of Carl Menger's. Von Weisser coined the term "marginal utility," and advanced the theory by considering disutility as well as utility.[54] An outgrowth of this was the concept of "opportunity cost." Any time resources are used in some capacity, the opportunity cost of their use is the utility or disutility of their use elsewhere. The opportunity cost of one hour's work is the utility associated with an hour's leisure. Thus the benefit of working

---
[51] J. B. Clark, "The Distribution of Wealth," in Charles W. Needy, op. cit., p. 148.
[52] Ibid.
[53] Ibid.
[54] Everett J. Burtt, Jr., op cit., p. 176.

(after-tax wages) must exceed the opportunity cost to justify the effort.

Clearly, this concept of opportunity cost is crucial to the supply side analysis. In fact, the entire marginalist contribution is paramount to modern microeconomic price theory. It sets the stage for the contributions of the neoclassicists regarding the determination of economic efficiency and welfare.

Alfred Marshall

Probably the most influential economist during the latter part of the nineteenth century and early portion of the twentieth century was Alfred Marshall, who was associated with the neoclassical school of economic analysis. His most famous work was *Principles of Economics*, published in 1890. Marshall defended the contributions of the classical economists, but incorporated marginalist principles; thus he provided a unified theory of value, incorporating marginal utility on the one hand, and costs on the other.[55]

Marshall was influenced by Charles Darwin's *Origin of Species*. Although he quarrelled with the Social Darwinists, he believed that the development of an economy was a slow, evolutionary process, not one subject to quantum leaps. In fact, the slogan for *Principles of Economics* was "Natura non facit satum," or nature does not leap.[56] The best vehicle for this evolutionary process—the only vehicle that would not retard technological progress—was the free market system.

Marshall's father intended for him to have a career in religion despite his obvious talents in the field of mathematics. But, Marshall went to Cambridge and obtained a degree in mathematics anyway. His religious upbringing, however, continued to affect him, and, in fact, he turned to economics as a means to consider ethical questions.[57] In Marshall's view, economics "is on the one side a study of wealth; and on the other, and more important side, a part of the study of man."[58] He reasoned that "man's character has been moulded by his everyday work,"[59] and the returns to effort "more than by any other influence unless it be that of his religious ideals."[60]

Marshall's work is permeated with tremendous optimism about the possibility of eradicating poverty. He wondered if it was time "to inquire whether it is necessary that there should be any so-called 'lower classes' at all."[61] To Marshall, poverty was degrading to the nation,

---

[55] Everett J. Burtt, Jr., op cit., p. 202.
[56] Alfred Marshall, *Principles of Economics*, (London: MacMillan and Company, Ltd., 1964), pp. xiii, 248-49.
[57] Everett J. Burtt, Jr., op. cit., p. 203.
[58] Alfred Marshall, op. cit., p. 1.
[59] *Ibid.*, p. 1.
[60] *Ibid.*
[61] *Ibid.*, p. 3.

and it was technological progress that provided the means for eliminating poverty:

> This progress has done more than anything else to give practical interest to the question whether it is really impossible that all should start in the world with a fair chance of leading a cultured life, free from the pains of poverty and the stagnating influences of excessive mechanical toil; and this question is being pressed to the front by the growing earnestness of age.[62]

Enterprise drew as much bad press in Marshall's time as it does today. Noting that the "term 'competition' has gathered about it evil savour,"[63] Marshall wrote that the positive side of the modern era is "a certain independence and habit of choosing one's course for oneself, a self-reliance,"[64] echoing the teachings of Adam Smith. Marshall also reiterated that it is "Freedom of Industry and Enterprise, or more shortly, Economic Freedom"[65] that yields the greatest potential for economic growth.

Marshall made several seminal contributions to economics and revised and up-dated some existing concepts. Several of them have a direct bearing on modern supply side economics and will be described here.

Any contemporary reader of economic literature might notice the heavy use of economic buzzwords. Marshall spent many chapters assigning carefully thought-out definition to words common in the economists' lexicon. He reaffirmed concepts of diminishing marginal utility of consumption and applied them directly to rigorous analysis of consumer demand.

Diminishing marginal utility implies, again, that as additional units are consumed, less satisfaction will be derived. This implies that an individual would be willing to pay less and less for additional units. If offered one hamburger, a hungry man will pay a certain price equal to the value he places on that hamburger. A second unit will not yield the same utility and thus the consumer would not pay as much. Additional hamburgers will be worth even less to him. The concept of diminishing marginal utility, then, directly implies the spector of negatively sloped demand curves—more is demanded only at lower prices. From this concept, Marshall developed a measure of the overall welfare of an individual and the basis for later quantification of the effects of taxes on that welfare. This measure became known as the "consumer surplus."

---

[62]*Ibid.*, p. 4.
[63]*Ibid.*, p. 6.
[64]*Ibid.*, p. 5.
[65]*Ibid.*, p. 10.

As stated by both the marginalists and Marshall, a given commodity will be consumed up to the point where the additional satisfaction derived (marginal utility) just equals the price of the unit of the commodity. Suppose this occurs at the point where ten units are consumed: This implies that the value assigned to the consumption of that tenth unit just equals the price. But given the concept of diminishing marginal utility, we know that the values of units one through nine are at least the same, and probably higher than that of the tenth, and yet, since the market will bear only one price for a given commodity, units one through nine cost less than they were valued — their marginal utilities exceeded their price. Thus, the consumers total expenditure (the price of each unit times the quantity purchased) is less than he would actually be willing to pay:

> We have already seen that the price which a person pays for a thing can never exceed, and seldom comes up to that which he would be willing to pay rather than go without it: so that the satisfaction which he gets from its purchase generally exceeds that which he gives up in paying away its price; and he thus derives from the purchase a surplus of satisfaction. The excess of the price which he would be willing to pay rather than go without the thing, over that which he actually does pay, is the economic measure of this surplus satisfaction. It may be called consumer's surplus.[66]

Clearly, if an individual is willing to pay much more for a quantity of a good then he actually has to, he is very well off indeed. Thus, the consumer surplus presents a measure of how well off an individual is. To make the concept clearer, consider an example provided by Marshall. "Let us take the case of a man, who, if the price of tea were 20s. a pound, would just be induced to buy one pound annually, . . ."[67]; he would buy two pounds if the price were 14s., three at 10s., four at 6s., five at 4s., six at 3s., and seven at 2s. Given a price of 2s., the consumer actually purchases seven pounds. But note that the "fact that he would just be induced to purchase one pound if the price were 20s., proves that the total enjoyment or satifaction which he derives from that pound is as great as that which he could obtain by spending 20s. on other things."[68] Similarly, each unit is worth (in terms of satisfaction) what he would be willing to pay for it. Since he would have, at 14s., bought two pounds, the marginal unit is worth exactly that amount. Thus his total enjoyment is the sum of the marginal utilities or 20s. + 14s. + 10s. + 6s. + 4s. + 3s. + 2s. = 59s. But he only had to pay 14s. for the whole lot. Thus his consumer surplus

---

[66] *Ibid.*, p. 124.
[67] *Ibid.*, p. 125.
[68] *Ibid.*

is 45s.; "he derives this 45s. worth of surplus enjoyment from his conjuncture."[69]

Clearly, society as a whole is better off the higher is the total of surplus value. This measure, then, also provides a means of quantifying the effects of taxes. In Marshall's previous example we can add an excise tax on tea of, say, 4s. Now the price increases to 6s. and the consumer will purchase four pounds. The total value to the consumer is 20s. + 14s. + 10s. + 6s. = 50s., and his expenditure is 24s. Because of the tax, the consumer surplus has dropped from 45s. to 26s.; that is, solely because of the implementation of the tax, total enjoyment has decreased.

This concept can be applied to any economic activity or the purchase of any commodity; it can apply to the use of production inputs as well consumption. Thus, it is a powerful tool indeed, and has been used widely in analyses of the effects of government actions on economic well being.

It is one thing to state that economic behavior will change in one direction or another due to government actions, but it is quite another to say by how much. Thus, Marshall's introduction of a "coefficient of elasticity" represents an important development. An elasticity is a numerical measure of the proportionate change in one thing caused by a proportionate change in something else. If one wonders how consumers will respond to a change in oil prices, an elasticity will provide the answer. Much of the debate over the recent tax legislation revolved around the responsiveness of investors and workers to after-tax rewards. Thus, the "elasticity of labor supply with respect to after-tax wages" and the "elasticity of saving with respect to after-tax rates of return" are crucial concepts, and it was Marshall who introduced the methodology by which we quantify this responsiveness to price changes.

Today, the responsiveness of saving to rates of return is a hotly debated topic, but in Marshall's day, it was a foregone conclusion that saving varied directly with after-tax rewards. Saving was viewed in terms of deferred consumption in that "the accumulation of wealth is generally the result of a postponement of enjoyment, or of a *waiting* for it."[70] And saving was considered to be interest elastic: "an increase in the future pleasure which can be secured by a present given sacrifice will in general increase the amount of present sacrifice that people will make."[71] Marshall allows for exceptions but notes that "none the less is it true that a fall in the distant benefits to be got by a

---

[69]*Ibid.*, p. 127.
[70]*Ibid.*, p. 233.
[71]*Ibid.*, p. 234.

given amount of working and waiting for the future does tend on the whole to diminish the provision which people make for the future; or in more modern phrase, that a fall in the rate of interest tends to check the accumulation of wealth."[72]

In Marshall's writing is seen a more sophisticated explanation of the market mechanism and the role of prices in resource allocation. For the pricing mechanism to work, of course, the market has to be relatively unencumbered, but in Marshall's time, as today, economists argued vehemently about the efficacy of market allocation versus government allocation. Marshall strongly believed that only the market could guarantee innovation and that excessive government intrusion "would deaden the energies of mankind, and arrest economic progress.[73]

Vilfredo Pareto

Economic theory can be characterized as either "positive" or "normative." Normative theory incorporates subjective social valuations, whereas positive theory is purely scientific and ethically neutral. Positive theory would be concerned with, say, the method by which output is maximized; the normative question would be whether such a process is desirable.

A major contribution in the area of positive economics came from the neoclassical writer Vilfredo Pareto, whose most famous writing concerns questions of economic efficiency. In much of the literature on the efficiency effects of taxes, the "Pareto Optimum" is the ideal against which the effects are measured.

Pareto was born in Paris and educated at the Polytechnical School of the University of Turin. He started his professional career as a businessman, but retired from those exploits at the age of thirty-four. At this point, Pareto pursued studies in history, philosophy, and economics and began a correspondence with Leon Walras. Pareto assumed Walras' professorship at Lausanne in 1893 and, though his views would diverge from Walras', he continued to use Walras' general equilibrium framework.[74]

Pareto objected to the interjection of normative social values into economics which he observed in the writings of many of his contemporaries. To him economics was a science and, thus, the primary questions of his discipline should concern economic efficiency.

Although he, too, incorporated marginalism into his analysis (his word for utility was "ophelimity"), he argued against certain economists who contended that the marginal value for a good could be determined in isolation, ignoring the rest of the economy. Pareto in-

---

[72]*Ibid.*, p. 235.
[73]*Ibid.*, p. 713.
[74]Everett J. Burtt, Jr., op. cit., pp. 257–59, 265–67.

sisted on a general equilibrium framework which stated that the value of an incremental unit was dependent upon events in the entire economy. A tenth unit of coffee may yield a certain level of satisfaction in the presence of sufficient quantities of milk and sugar, but that same unit may produce an entirely different amount of utility should something drastic happen in sugar and dairy markets.

This emphasis on general equilibrium effects is crucial to supply side analysis. Consider, for example, the case of tax equity. Traditionally, equity has been judged by the initial incidence of a tax, rather than the incidence after the effects of the tax have rippled through the economy. The conventional wisdom would hold that a very high rate of tax on capital is equitable, considering the "ability to pay" definition of equity, because more rich people than poor people own capital. But it is altogether possible that rich people can shift their investments out of a highly taxed country to the point where their costs are minimized and they enjoy about the same rates of return. The absence of capital in the highly taxed country will lead to unemployment and a decrease in the real wage rate; that is, workers will bear a high burden from the capital levy. Thus, a tax that initially appeared equitable may, when viewed in a general equilibrium setting, actually be regressive.

Virtually every article in the Public Finance literature involving the effects of government actions on efficient resource allocation identifies a set of "Pareto optimality" conditions by which to judge such actions. In fact, the heart of supply side economics is the desire to raise government revenue in a way that least distorts resource composition. Pareto's contribution in the area of allocative economics is, therefore, crucial.

In the model used by Pareto, individuals attempt to maximize their own welfare and firms try to maximize their profits. Each economic actor has a set of tastes or preferences but is constrained by a set of "obstacles." The question is: What will lead to "maximum ophelimity," or economic efficiency, a situation defined by a stable equilibrium?

Pareto's definition of economic efficiency has stood the test of time:

> We will say that the members of a collectivity enjoy maximum ophelimity in a certain position when it is impossible to find a way of moving from that position very slightly in such a manner that the ophelimity enjoyed by each of the individuals of that collectivity increases or decreases. That is to say, any small displacement in departing from that position necessarily has the effect of increasing the ophelimity which certain individuals enjoy, and decreasing that which others enjoy, of being agreeable to some and disagreeable to others.[75]

---
[75]Vilfredo Pareto, *Manual of Political Economy*, (Augustus M. Kelley, 1971), p. 201.

The question above can be rephrased to ask: What situation will lead to the case where no one individual can be made better off unless another is made worse off?

How individuals maximize their welfare under constraint has been discussed in previous sections. Given a limited income, an individual should allocate his expenditures so that the additional satisfaction from each good, weighted by the price of each good, is equal: To reach an optimum, the benefits from each good should be the same. In production, similarly, the marginal cost of production should equal the marginal benefit, and the marginal output from each factor input should be the same. But what will determine these conditions? In Pareto's view:

> ...tastes, and the consideration of the existing quantities of certain goods, determine the relationships between prices and quantities sold or purchased. Furthermore, the theory of production tells us that, given these relationships, the quantities and the prices are determined. The problem of equilibrium is thus completely solved.[76]

Thus, if tastes can be freely expressed, the pricing mechanism yields an equilibrium. And it is competition that guarantees the optimal solution:

> Free competition determines the coefficients of production in a way that assures maximum ophelimity. It tends to equalize the net income of such capital as can be created by means of saving, indeed, savings obviously are transformed into that capital yielding the most income.[77]

To Pareto, any equilibrium reached through competition resulted in the highest level of societal welfare. But Pareto feared that, even in free enterprise systems, government would interfere with competition. He saw his world as distorted by greed and monopoly, encouraged by government which he saw as "insatiable; as its power wanes, its fraudulent practices increase."[78]

Other Neoclassicists

The neoclassical period produced a wealth of contributions on resource allocation, social welfare, value, and income distribution. As in any period, there were intellectual disagreements among those describing themselves as neoclassicists, but much of the modern theory stems from this era.

Pareto insisted on complete ethical neutrality in economics. Arthur Cecil Pigou, on the other hand, was devoted to somewhat more nor-

---

[76]*Ibid.*, p. 260.
[77]*Ibid.*, p. 266.
[78]Vilfredo Pareto, *The Rise and Fall of the Elites*, quoted in Everett J. Burtt, Jr., op. cit., p. 275.

mative concerns—the determinants of maximum social selfare. Pigou was a student of Marshall and a member of the Cambridge School of Economics. Considered the father of modern welfare economics, Pigou's most famous work was *The Economics of Welfare*. In this book Pigou established criteria by which to judge the welfare of a nation. Pigou argued that the national dividend (equivalent to net national product) is the proper measure of welfare, and carefully described how it could be maximized.

Given a certain endowment of resources, how can they be allocated so as to maximize the national dividend? The contribution of an additional unit of some input is, in Pigou's terms, defined as the net social product of that input. Pigou argues that "only one arrangement of resources will make the values of marginal net products everywhere equal."[79] But such an arrangement is desirable:

> It follows that, since, *ex hypothesi,* there is only one arrangement of resources that will make the values of the marginal social net products equal in all uses, this arrangement is necessarily the one that makes the national dividend, as defined here, a maximum.[80]

Why is this so? If resources are allocated so that the marginal contribution of one resource is greater than that of another, output could be increased simply by reallocating resources towards the more productive inputs. If I have a limited amount of money to pay laborers, and, say, all wages are the same, I will hire the most productive workers. In fact, I will allocate my money until the marginal contributions from all are the same because, should the marginal contribution from one worker be less, I would hire someone else. Of course, Pigou's criterion is an extention of the Pareto efficiency requirements discussed earlier.

Out of the classical, marginalist, and neoclassical writers has evolved a unified theory of value, production, allocation, and distribution. People make decisions on the basis of their appraisal of the marginal costs and marginal benefits of certain activities. Further, prices serve to allocate resources to different uses. This makes it possible to define the way in which resources should be allocated so as to maximize economic welfare. And finally, it is possible to state that, if the market system functions correctly, prices will allocate resources to their most valued uses. The neoclassical economist Philip H. Wicksteed expressed this aptly:

> The market tends to establish an identity of the place of differential value of any commodity amongst all exchangeable things on every-

---

[79]A. C. Pigou, *The Economics of Welfare*, (MacMillan and Co., Ltd., 1950), p. 136.
[80]*Ibid.*

body's scale of preferences, and further to secure that it is higher on the scale of every one that has it than on the scale of any one who has it not; so that to that extent, and in that sense, things must always tend to go and stay where they are most significant.[81]

This brings us to the modern period. In a properly functioning economy, prices are crucial to the efficient allocation of resources. Anything that distorts prices or costs can have a decided effect on economic health. Thus, the way in which government taxing and spending policies affect relative prices and costs at the margin is crucial, and, in fact, the modern neoclassical theory of Public Finance is concerned with just this issue. And, as should be clear, the policy precepts associated with the new supply side economics are an outgrowth of neoclassical Public Finance theory.

The Modern Period

In the postwar period two parallel bodies of Public Finance thinking have flourished, both utilizing neoclassical techniques. Not surprisingly, one body is concerned with the expenditure side of the budget and the other with the taxing side. The former is popularly known as the "Public Choice" literature, while the latter I will characterize as the "optimal taxation" literature. The basic questions addressed by these two groups are: 1) What is the optimal level of government provision relative to private provision? and 2) Given a level of government expenditure, what is the least distorting method of finance?

In the Public Choice literature it is assumed that some role for government exists, given certain failures of the market, and the trick is to allocate resources between private and public uses so as to maximize efficiency (in the literature this point is referred to as the Lindahl Solution). The Lindahl Solution is Pareto Optimal; that is, Public Choice economists have sought to determine Pareto Optimality conditions for government expenditures. This subject is dealt with at length elsewhere in this volume, so a thorough exposition would be redundant. But the recent supply side policy suggestions indicate that government expenditures should be reduced. This stems directly from the belief that the level of public provision relative to private provision is super-optimal, and hence, that the economy is operating inefficiently. Referring back to the teachings of Pareto, this means that, by reallocating resources, society can be made better off. Since the economy is operating inefficiently some people can be made better off without making anyone else worse off by reallocating

---

[81]Philip H. Wicksteed, "The Scope and Method of Political Economy in the Light of the 'Marginal' Theory of Value and Distribution," reprinted in Charles W. Needy, op. cit., pp. 257–258.

resources towards the private sector. Thus, the desire to cut government expenditures is a direct result of an interpretation of mainstream neoclassical public finance theory.

Long before the term "supply side economics" was coined, economists studied the effects of taxes on prices and hence resource allocation. In his seminal work on investment theory, Dale W. Jorgenson stated:

> The central feature of the neoclassical theory is the response of the demand for capital to changes in relative factor prices.[82]

In later work with Robert E. Hall, Jorgenson presented empirical evidence that investment was responsive to tax treatment.[83] Reams have been written on the responsiveness of savers and workers to tax treatment, but as this work will be covered extensively elsewhere in this volume, it need not be discussed here. Arnold Harberger made a seminal contribution on the way in which differential taxes contribute to inefficiency. Utilizing concepts originating with Marshall and Walras, he estimated the loss of efficiency associated with the corporate income tax.[84]

The more recent literature under the optimal taxation heading specifically considers the best way to raise a given level of revenue. As Agnar Sandmo has pointed out, this literature judges taxes with respect to their departure from Pareto optimal conditions.[85]

Supply side economists have stressed that the tax reforms suggested recently should be judged not by the extent that they increase demand (the Keynesian view) but by the extent that they reduce the aggregate drag on the economy by the distorting effect of taxes (the neoclassical view). Thus the policy suggestions of the supply side school are fully compatable with the spirit of the huge body of optimal taxation literature.

Finally, one must consider the reform of a tax system which implies a revenue loss within the context of budget constraints. Do deficits matter? Are they inflationary? Do tax cuts in and of themselves increase perceptions of wealth or aggregate demand? These topics are considered in other essays in this volume, but suffice it to say

---

[82]Dale W. Jorgenson, "Capital Theory and Investment Behavior," Proceedings, *American Economic Association* (May 1962), p. 247.

[83]Dale W. Jorgenson and Robert E. Hall, "Application of the Theory of Optimum Capital Accumulation," in *Tax Incentives and Capital Spending*, Gary Fromm, editor, (Washington, D.C.: The Brookings Institution, 1967), pp. 17–18.

[84]Arnold C. Harberger, "The Measurement of Waste," *American Economic Review* (May 1964). "Corporation Income Taxes," in *Taxation and Welfare*; "The Incidence of the Corporate Income Tax," in *Journal of Political Economy* (June 1962).

[85]Agnar Sandmo, "Optimal Taxation: An Introduction to the Literature," *Journal of Public Economy* (August 1976), pp. 37–54.

that respected mainstream writers such as Martin Bailey and Robert Barro have reinforced the view expressed by Norman Ture.[86]

A Note on Markets and Keynesians

The supply side or neoclassical mode of analysis takes as a prerequisite the efficient functioning of markets. Given such markets, interference in the form of unwarranted government intrusion reduces growth and general wellbeing. The Keynesian mode of analysis disputes the existence of efficient markets. In the Keynesian view, the world is characterized by sticky prices that do not adjust to represent value and widespread money illusion (economic actors cannot differentiate between real and nominal values). Since markets don't function according to this view, government intervention is necessary to allocate resources to their best uses.

Any theory based on money illusion is intellectually unsatisfying at best. Why should it be that certain individuals are constantly fooled because of money illusion? And yet the pure neoclassical world of perfect foresight and instantaneous adjustment seems equally implausible.

A new body of literature, alternatively referred to as the "New Classical" or "rational expectations" school, offers an intellectually satisfying reconciliation between neoclassical analysis and the observation that institutional factors cause lags affecting price adjustment. This is covered extensively in another essay in this book. But after explicitly incorporating information costs into the framework, the neoclassical analysis proves to be valid, and Keynesian theories of continuing disequilibrium are rejected. Thus, the modern economy can be characterized as one in which prices do reflect value and do effect the efficient allocation of resources. This analysis actually reveals another aspect of the way in which government actions influence relative prices. By introducing government-induced uncertainty, tax and spending actions exacerbate price differentiality over and above what would occur in a world where the future was known with certainty.

Conclusion

The passage of the Reagan administration's economic program represents a momentous occasion in the economic history of this nation—momentous because no one would argue that it does not represent a shift with regard to the philosophy of the role of government in the economy.

During the decades following World War II economic policy came

---

[86] Robert Barro, "Are Government Bonds Net Wealth?" *Journal of Political Economy* (November/December 1974).

to be based on the theories of the so-called neoclassical-Keynesian synthesis, which implied a large role for government. Given that the macroeconomic theory that gave birth to these policies has permeated our universities, the press, and the political arena for years, it is not surprising that there is a great deal of confusion over the Reagan program and its underpinnings. The analytical tools utilized by economists of the Paul Samuelson era simply don't fit with a market system. This is complicated further because political needs often obscure the economic content of a program.

The problem of analyzing supply side policies with Keynesian tools is one thing, but when political motives come into play as well it becomes impossible to carry out a rational debate. George F. Will is fond of saying that reasonable men can disagree, and this is certainly true in the field of economics. But misrepresentation of theories is unacceptable. We can disagree reasonably about assumptions, empirical matters, and policy prescriptions as long as the issues are being properly stated.

The definition of supply side economics given at the beginning of this essay is, I feel, the most correct since it is the most representative of those economists in and out of government who are currently affecting policy. The purpose of this essay is not to convince the reader of the efficacy of supply side policies, but rather to illustrate that, given the best definition of the theory behind them, one can trace the roots to a consistent, logical, traditional body of literature that is readily accepted in university teaching on the micro-level. It is not a new miracle cure for economic ills, but rather the result of over two hundred years of evolution in economic thinking.

RATIONAL EXPECTATIONS AND SUPPLY SIDE ECONOMICS: MATCH OR MISMATCH?

by

DAVID G. TUERCK

Formerly with the American Enterprise Institute, Dr. Tuerck is now a Director in the Economic Studies Group of the Management Consulting Services practise of Coopers & Lybrand in Washington, D.C.

PROGRESS IN ECONOMICS, AS IN OTHER DISCIPLINES, IS NOT always the result of organized effort to bring about a preconceived result. As in the laboratory or factory, where new ideas about how to design or improve a product can spring up by accident, the Washington policy environment will occasionally force a synthesis of seemingly disparate ideas about how to go about analyzing economic activity. An example was offered by the revelation in early 1981 that the Reagan Administration had turned to a relatively unknown econometric model to forecast the effects of the economic policy changes it was about to undertake. This model, offered by the Claremont Economics Institute, was described in the press as a challenge to the established models offered by Data Resources, Chase Econometrics, Wharton Econometric Forecasting Associates, and other well-known vendors. According to one account, the Claremont model won attention at a time when the forecasting record of other econometric models was becoming increasingly suspect. Moreover, according to this account, Office of Management and Budget Director David Stockman and other Administration officials felt that the established models were at odds with the intellectual underpinnings of Administration policy. "It was, of course, never in the cards that such a committed supply sider as Stockman would depend on one of the big three models to predict the consequences of Reagan's 'New Beginning'."[1]

While details of the Claremont model have not, apparently, been made public, it is possible to surmise some of its distinguishing characteristics. Reportedly, for example, the Claremont model differs from the established models insofar as it embodies "rational," rather than "adaptive," expectations. The idea of adaptive expectations is:

> that people make their judgment about the future direction of prices from the slow accumulation of experience at the grocery store and the

---

[1] *Business Week*, March 30, 1981, p. 71. As this volume neared publication, Stockman had begun to cast doubt on the strength of his commitment. The strength of the Administration's commitment, however, appeared to be undiminished.

gas station. The alternative theory—"rational expectations"—holds that individual price forecasts tend to be made on the basis of a relatively rapid judgment about the future direction of monetary and fiscal policies.[2]

With this revelation, the question arises whether rational expectations as such (that is, apart from its embodiment in any particular, proprietary model) offers a viable approach to forecasting economic activity. Is rational expectations, as one account put it, "implicitly embodied in supply side forecasts"?[3]

This paper offers some judgments on these issues. The analysis begins with an exposition of supply side economics and continues with a discussion of the evolution of rational expectations as a school of thought. The overriding issue, from which it is hoped that the analysis will derive a unifying theme, is whether supply side economics and rational expectations have an intellectual kinship that provides the basis for generally improving the way people think about economic activity. As viewed here, that issue has two parts. The first part (and the one occupying most of the pages that follow) has to do with whether the behavioral premises underlying rational expectations do or do not complement those underlying supply side economics. The second part has to do with the more difficult question whether policies based on rational expectations are likely to succeed. To what extent do such policies presuppose, perhaps unrealistically, that people are willing to trust policy makers to adhere to a policy line that is itself rational?

Supply Side Economics: Background and Summary

In attacking these issues, it is useful first to review some of the fundamental tenets of supply side economics. As the reader will no doubt learn as he proceeds through this volume, the idea of supply side economics is part slogan and part economics. The part that is slogan is meant to underscore the one-sided nature of the once established and now largely disestablished Keynesian approach to economic theory. Keynes, his disciples, and the establishment models of the sixties and seventies stressed the importance of aggregate demand in determining the pace of real and nominal economic activity. Their drawback is that they neglected the role of supply, meaning all of the factors that enter into people's decisions to offer their services for use in production. While all economists (Keynesian and non-Keynesian) recognized the role of efficient markets in providing for the

---

[2]*Ibid.*, p. 71.
[3]"Supply-Side Economics Commands New Respect," *New York Times*, March 5, 1981, p. D 14.

supply of productive services, most economists (in particular the Keynesians) stressed the importance, and the separability from supply considerations, of aggregate demand. Thus, the leading textbooks (indeed, whole college curricula) implied that the study of aggregate (or "macro") economics was the study of aggregate demand. The factors affecting aggregate supply did not, in and of themselves, have much to do with the performance of the economy as a whole.

By the nineteen-seventies, however, this tradition was under siege. It had, for one, been shaken by the monetarist revolution, led by Milton Friedman and discussed below, which challenged the capacity of the Keynesian framework for explaining economic change. More seriously, perhaps, the onset of stagflation undermined the perceived practical value of the Keynesian models for forecasting economic activity or for guiding economic policy. One set of reactions to this turn of events consisted, as we shall see, of a series of refinements in the monetarist revolution already underway. It is this set of refinements that came to be described as the rational expectations approach. Another set of reactions consisted of reopening the broader question whether the whole idea of aggregate demand, as embodied in the Keynesian framework, provides an acceptable conceptualization. Perhaps the Keynesian models were failing, not because they emphasized the wrong determinants of aggregate demand (government spending, as opposed to the money supply), but because they ignored the conditions affecting the supply of productive services.

The Keynesian Background

Although this helps explain why the expression supply side economics became a convenient slogan, it also shows how the slogan can be misleading. The reason is that both Keynesian and supply side frameworks embody supply and demand concepts. Both attempt to explain aggregate economic activity on the basis of what are determined or believed to be the underlying supply and demand conditions. With respect to the Keynesian framework, these conditions include prior restrictions on the behavior of nominal wage rates and certain claims concerning the responsiveness of investment to interest rates, the responsiveness of interest rates to the money supply, and the role of savings in determining capital formation.[4]

According to Keynes, nominal wages can always rise, but numerous institutional barriers keep them from falling or, if they do fall, from increasing aggregate demand and, therefore, employment. In-

---

[4]John Maynard Keynes, *The General Theory of Employment, Interest, and Money*, (London-New York: MacMillan, 1936).

sofar as employers' demands for labor vary inversely with real wages, it is impractical or ineffective to expect workers to accept lower nominal wages in exchange for more jobs. The practical remedy is to increase aggregate demand and prices through government spending. Workers who will not offer their services at reduced real wage rates brought about by reduced nominal wage rates will do so at reduced real wage rates brought about by increased prices. Too low a level of aggregate demand will cause "involuntary unemployment" of the kind experienced during the Great Depression.

The idea that workers will systematically ignore the effects of higher prices on real wages is a form of what has come to be known as "money illusion." The same idea is present in the evidence, offered by A. W. Phillips, of an inverse relationship between unemployment and rates of change of nominal wages.[5] Employers bid nominal wages up or down with increases or decreases in aggregate demand. Workers respond by offering more or less of their services irrespective of price changes. On the assumption that prices are some markup over nominal wages and therefore move in the same direction as nominal wages, there exists a "Phillips curve" tradeoff between inflation and unemployment: the more inflation we are willing to suffer, the less unemployment we have to suffer. It is this tradeoff by which the major econometric models came to be identified—and, some would argue, discredited—during the nineteen-seventies.

Two additional empirical claims enter into the Keynesian theory of involuntary unemployment. One of these—absolute liquidity preference—holds that there is a certain floor below which interest rates will not fall. Above this floor, the monetary authorities can raise or lower interest rates by lowering or raising the quantity of money in the hands of the public. But once interest rates have reached the point of absolute liquidity preference, further increases in the money supply will fail to bring about reductions in interest rates. If, for example, the central bank engages in open market purchases of government securities, the public will simply exchange the securities for cash without increasing their expenditures. There will be no stimulus to demand either directly or indirectly through reduced interest rates. The second empirical claim is that, even within the range over which interest rates will respond to money supply changes, business investment will tend to be insensitive to the changes in interest rates that the monetary authorities are able to

---

[5] A. W. Phillips, "The Relationship between Unemployment and the Rate of Change of Money Wage Rates in the United Kingdom," *Economica*, XXV (November, 1958) pp. 283–299.

bring about. "Monetary policy is twice damned."[6] Money supply increases offer no escape from a deep contraction because they offer little scope for lowering interest rates or, inasmuch as they do bring about lower interest rates, increasing business investment. The only recourse, then, is price and demand increases through increased government spending.

This line of reasoning led to the formulation of certain policy multipliers that were claimed to translate changes in government spending into resulting changes in output and prices. The ability of policy makers to use government spending as a reliable tool for conducting economic stabilization policy depends on the fourth leg of Keynes' argument—that private saving is in no sense a determinant of capital formation but merely a residual, the amount left over after consumption, to finance business investment and any excess of government spending over taxes. Once the individual "propensity to save" was known, the government could predict the impact of an additional dollar of net spending on national income. If the economy was below full employment, that impact would consist mainly of an increase in real national income by some calculable multiple of the increase in the deficit. If it was at full employment, the increase in national income would be in nominal terms only.

Government therefore had at once an opportunity and a responsibility. The opportunity arose from the reliability with which it could forecast the effects of business investment and government spending on aggregate economic activity. The Keynesian "multiplier" would provide a convenient tool for understanding how fiscal policy and monetary policy, through its effects on investment, would impact the economy. The responsibility consisted of overcoming past taboos against deficit spending and, especially in depressed times, of not relying on monetary policy or business investment to put things right. At first, then, government deficits were seen as a cure for the Great Depression. Later on, with the estimation of the Phillips curve and the development of the major econometric models, enlightened economic policy was seen as a matter of fine tuning—of striking the proper tradeoff between full employment and price stability.

The Supply Side Response

The supply side response to this set of developments has focused on the logical and empirical underpinnings of Keynesian underemployment. Supply side economics rejects the idea of Keynesian-type money illusion as illogical: why should workers respond any differ-

---

[6]Milton Friedman, "The Role of Monetary Policy," Presidential Address before the American Economic Association, Washington, D.C., December 29, 1967, in *American Economic Review*, 58 (March, 1968), p. 2.

ently to real wage changes brought about by price level changes than to real wage changes brought about by nominal wage changes? By failing to offer a satisfactory answer, Keynes failed to demonstrate the possibility of involuntary unemployment. By treating the saving-investment nexus as he did, he lured future generations of economists and policy makers into a combination of logical and factual error that has manifested itself in the form of escalating inflation and falling potential real growth.

The supply side attack on Keynes does not deny the existence of a link between economic policy, including fiscal policy, and the level of output and employment. Rather it defines that link according to the effects of economic policy on relative prices. Absent any taxes, workers would adjust the quantity of their services that they offer employers according to the nominal wage that employers are willing to pay, relative to the price of goods. Employers would adjust their demand for workers' services according to the nominal wages at which workers offered their services, relative to the price of goods and relative to the prices of other inputs. Savers would adjust the amount of consumption they were willing to forgo now according to the size of the income stream they would be able to capture by purchasing a given asset, relative to its purchase price. The appropriate role of economic policy, in this light, is to identify and, as far as possible, reduce any relative price distortions that might discourage employers from using the services of labor and capital. Although other such distortions exist and are easily identified, taxes are a leading culprit. More to the point, the only meaningful gauge of tax policy and of economic policy in general is its capacity to widen or narrow the relative price distortions that dampen people's willingness to buy each other's goods and services.

Keynes erred because he failed to show that distortions in relative prices could bring about involuntary unemployment of the kind he sought to cure. Keynesian money illusion does not offer a credible demonstration. Having failed to explain involuntary unemployment, Keynes created an analytical framework that was rigged, in a sense, to worsen it. By excluding from consideration the effects of taxes on relative prices and by creating an artificial distinction between saving and investment, he revealed and, as it turned out, bequeathed to later generations a mindset that was insensitive to the effects of tax changes on supplies of productive services.

Taxes distort relative prices by forming a wedge between the price offered by buyers and the price received by sellers. Taxes discourage employment by forcing the worker to hand over to government part of the wage employers offer for his services. They discourage saving by forcing the saver, similarly, to part with some of the future income that is made possible by his willingness to forgo some consumption now in exchange for more consumption later. The goal of fiscal policy is to satisfy the resource needs of government in a way that imposes the least burden on people's willingness to work and save. Policies aimed at maintaining some ideal level of aggregate demand are, at best, misplaced and, at worst, likely to increase this burden.

Norman Ture, one of the most eloquent exponents of this point of view, notes that:

> the phrase "supply side economics" really is a misnomer. It suggests, incorrectly, that this analytical approach is distinguished from the more conventional analyses by its effects on supply rather than demand conditions. In fact, however, the actual distinction is that "supply side" analysis identifies the initial effects of a tax or other fiscal actions in terms of what it does to one or another relative price and seeks to describe and measure the responses of households and businesses to such relative price changes.[7]

The Keynesian framework is deficient in this respect for two reasons: first, because it identifies the initial effects of tax changes for their impact on disposable income, rather than relative prices, and second because it omits or confuses the effects of tax changes on investment. Tax rate decreases are not, in and of themselves, expansive or inflationary, because they cannot by themselves increase aggregate demand. No expansion in real output is possible, following a tax rate cut, until workers and savers discover that the after-tax return to increased work and saving has increased. The lower tax rates will bring about a fall in the amount of revenues that the government is able to collect from taxpayers (the extent of which will vary inversely with the supply response by workers and savers). But, unless the revenue shortfall is financed by money creation, the resulting increase in disposable income will, in and of itself, exert no upward effect on either real output or prices: people will merely use money that would otherwise have been paid out in taxes to buy government bonds.[8]

---

[7] *"Supply-Side" Economics and Public Policy*, Testimony presented to the Joint Economic Committee, Congress of the United States, May 21, 1980 (Washington, D.C.: Norman B. Ture, Inc. and Institute for Research on the Economics of Taxation, 1980), p. 3.

[8] This both opens and closes a number of arguments often raised about the likely effectiveness of tax cuts for generating real output increases. It closes one issue, namely, whether the "income effect" of increased after-tax wage rates (the fact that workers will feel richer and thus want more leisure) will offset the "substitution effect" (the inclination to take advantage of the higher after-tax wage rates by working harder). If there are no first-order income effects, then the only way that a tax cut can generate income effects is for workers to respond by substituting work for leisure. However, it opens a different issue, whether the government borrowing made necessary by a revenue shortfall will "crowd out" as much investment as the

The Keynesian framework confuses the effect of taxation on saving and investment by treating saving, first, as an act that can be separated from investment and, second, as a residual—the part of disposable income that remains after consumption. In contrast to "the aggregate demand models which include an investment function as an aggregate demand component and, as essentially, the exclusive province of business firms," supply side economics delineates investment

> as the effort to implement changes in the desired stocks of capital; since the function representing the desired stock of capital does not pertain to the business entity but to the population as a whole, investment behavior is not a separate activity from saving. It has the same determinants and is identically influenced by fiscal actions.[9]

In a supply side framework, saving is capital formation—the production of real income-earning assets. People save by directing productive services from the production of consumer goods to the production of capital goods. The only effect of taxes is to drive a wedge between the future income that will be thrown off by capital goods and the future income that savers can expect to enjoy in exchange for their forgoing consumption now. The lower the wedge, the greater that future income and, hence, the greater the incentive to save.

Thus presented, the supply side argument reduces to three observations about the importance of aggregate demand in government policy making.

1. In the absence of unnecessary interference by government (but assuming that necessary conditions for peaceful commerce—law and order, respect for contracts, and so forth—are present) supply and demand take care of themselves. Buyers and sellers fail to work out all the opportunities for productive effort and for mutually-beneficial exchange only insofar as taxes and other factors create distortions in relative prices. The lower these distortions, the greater the potential real growth of the economy.

2. Given whatever set of distortions that may be in existence, there is some underlying growth path along which the economy will tend to move, subject only to random disturbances. Changes in tax rates and other policy instruments will cause a shift in this path, de-

---

tax cut is able to bring about. The answer depends in part on the ability of the tax cut to expand output and, hence, people's willingness to forgo current consumption in exchange for government promises of future income streams. It also depends on people's expectations of and their response to the future tax liabilities that may be incurred to finance the additional debt issued now to finance a revenue shortfall.

[9]Norman B. Ture, *"Supply-Side" Economics and Public Policy*, p. 12.

pending on whether they succeed in widening or narrowing existing distortions (or introducing new ones) and depending on the response by savers and workers.

3. Government cannot increase real output directly by increasing aggregate demand. It can bring about price level increases or decreases by undertaking appropriately expansive or contractive monetary policies. Insofar as policies aimed at expanding or contracting aggregate demand end up increasing or decreasing the price level, they can succeed in exerting real output effects only insofar as they impact relative prices. One way that monetary policy does affect real output is through "bracket creep"—the tendency of inflation to drive income earners into higher tax brackets. The higher his tax bracket, the greater the amount of tax that the income earner must pay on an additional dollar earned and, hence, the greater the wedge between what his employer is willing to pay for an hour of his effort and the amount he receives. "Expansive" monetary policies thereby have the effect of reducing the incentive to work and the output of goods. Such policies are twice inflationary—once by raising prices at existing production levels and again by reducing the output of goods that people can buy at existing prices.

The idea that expansive monetary policy is likely to be associated with decreases in real output is for most economists, Keynesian and non-Keynesian, counterintuitive. Indeed, we shall see that post-Keynesian debate concerning the importance of monetary policy has centered on the strength and dependability of money supply increases for generating real output increases. Yet, supply side logic may be interpreted to lead to the conclusion that, as far as real output is concerned (bracket-creep aside), money does not matter:

> At the heart of this issue is whether monetary policy has any substantial bearing, even in the short run, on real economic activity—on supplies of factors of production, the rate of their utilization, or total real output. There is much in the developing "supply side" economics which argues that there is no significant relationship between changes in the pace of monetary growth and changes in real output and employment.[10]

Supply side economics is in part a rejection of simplistic rationalizations of underemployment equilibrium and in part a restatement of neoclassical price theory. It is not, as such—and, indeed, it argues against the very idea of—a theory of aggregate economic activity in which individual economic agents perceive and interpret the price of

---

[10]Norman B. Ture, "What Money Supply Doesn't Do," *The Wall Street Journal*, June 20, 1980. Reprinted by permission of The Wall Street Journal,© Dow Jones & Company, 1980. All rights reserved.

goods in general differently from the way they perceive and interpret the prices at which they are able to sell their own individual factor services in the markets for labor and capital. The question at issue here is how the tenets of supply side economics should be extended to the analysis of monetary policy and of the general price level. Are changes in the growth rate of money in fact unimportant except for their effects on the general price level? Do changes in the general price level brought about by money-supply changes always leave relative prices unchanged, bracket-creep aside? To what extent is it possible to accommodate, within the supply side framework, conventional ideas concerning the effects of money growth rates on real output?

Rational Expectations: Origin and Debate

The supply side approach to economics consists mainly, as we have seen, of a criticism of the logical underpinnings of Keynesian theory. Because there is no logical defense of money illusion or of conceptually distinct savings and investment decisions, there is no basis either for Keynesian explanations of economic behavior.

Beginning in the nineteen-fifties, well before the supply side ideas of today became fashionable, a group of economists, led by Milton Friedman and later to be called "monetarists," began to question Keynesian theory on different grounds. Whereas the supply side school would attack the logical underpinnings of Keynesianism, the monetarists attacked its ability to predict. The question raised by the monetarists was whether the quantity theory of money provides a better tool for predicting economic behavior than the Keynesian framework. While the monetarists, like supply siders, took it upon themselves to question the conceptual properties of the Keynesian framework, they did not set out directly to debunk that framework as merely illogical. Rather, in the spirit of Friedman's philosophy of science, they sought to refine — and, as needed, redefine — Keynesian theory and the quantity theory in such a way as to make them comparable but competing theories of economic behavior, testable according to which provides the better predictor of economic behavior.

As part of this process, it was desirable, but not necessary, to probe every assumption for its intuitive plausibility. The proof was, instead, in the evidence. According to the quantity theory, money is a principal determinant of economic activity. According to Keynesian theory, business investment and government purchases of goods and services (so-called autonomous expenditures) comprise a stronger and more reliable determinant. Much of the work of the monetarists has been aimed at testing this proposition by comparing cyclical behavior with the behavior of money and with the behavior of autonomous expenditures. Their finding that Keynes was wrong—that money offers the stronger and more reliable determinant—was at least equal in importance to the deficiencies that the supply siders were to expose later on. Keynes had set out to provide a radical explanation for the Great Depression in the face of the supposed failures of the then conventional economics. Friedman's empirical results suggested that Keynes' apparatus was less useful for explaining business cycles than a set of ideas that could be recognized in the writings of David Hume.

The Monetarist Revolution

Friedman laid out the elements of his theoretical approach in a 1956 article.[11] The quantity theory of money, as it has been nurtured and perfected by Friedman and his predecessors at the University of Chicago, rests on three premises:

1. *The demand for money is stable and can be expressed as a function of a limited number of variables.* This is to say that the quantity theory is indeed a "theory" and not just an identity. As an identity, the quantity theory says that the annual dollar volume of nominal income (or of transactions) must equal the money stock times the number of times the money stock turns over in a year. The frequency with which money turns over—its "velocity"—merely tells us how hard it must work to generate a given volume of nominal income. As a theory, the quantity theory holds that people's demand for money can be expressed as a reciprocal of its velocity and that the velocity tends to be well behaved (in the sense that it is stable and depends on a limited number of variables). As an identity, the quantity "theory" always holds true: the quantity of money held by people times the velocity of money must always equal the dollar value of nominal income received by them. As a theory, it adds the claim that, given any change in the quantity of money held by people, the burden is on nominal income, not velocity, to adjust in such a way as to satisfy the identity.

2. *People or business firms view money as a form of wealth or as a productive asset.* The money holder's demand for money depends on the services it performs, the cost of holding it, and the size and distribution between different asset types of the money holder's total wealth. Money is, in this sense, like any other commodity or factor of pro-

---

[11]"The Quantity Theory of Money: A Restatement," in *Studies in the Quantity Theory of Money*, ed. by Milton Friedman (Chicago: University of Chicago Press, 1956), reprinted in *The Optimum Quantity of Money and Other Essays* (Chicago: Aldine Publishing Company, 1969), pp. 50–67.

duction for which people's demands will vary inversely with cost and directly with total wealth or income.

3. *The supply of money depends on factors that are in essential respects separate from the factors that determine the demand for money.* Either there are physical or natural limitations on the quantity of money in existence (as under a commodity standard, such as gold), or the government has the power, if not the will, to place limits on money creation.

The demand for money is ordinarily, in this framework, expressed as a demand for real balances (that is nominal balances divided by an index of the price of goods in general). People determine their desired real balances according to the price of holding them (ordinarily the nominal return on income-earning assets), the size of their other wealth holdings (ordinarily represented by their real income), and other variables.

The Federal Reserve System determines the size of people's nominal cash balances through open market operations, loans to commercial banks, and adjustments in reserve requirements. When people experience a rise in their nominal cash balances, they find that their real cash balances are temporarily too large. They try to reduce their real balances by spending their nominal balances. But, because they are unable, in the aggregate, to reduce their nominal balances, they must find some different way to bring their actual real and nominal balances into line with their desired real and nominal balances. "Equilibrium" in this sense is achieved through a combination of adjustments in the price of goods, "the" nominal interest rate, and real income. As people try to spend down their nominal balances they will try to buy goods and income-earning assets. Insofar as they are able, in this process, to coax out more production of consumer and capital goods, they will succeed in driving up real income and driving down interest rates. They will, to that extent, be more content to hold the real balances actually in their possession. The remainder of the adjustment must come through an increase in the price of goods great enough to bring actual real balances into line with desired real balances.

The core issue for supply siders in this scenario has to do, as we have seen, with the possibility of short-run real output increases. The core issue for Keynesians has to do with the possibility of either real output or price increases in response to money-supply changes.

If money holders exhibit "absolute liquidity preference" in the sense explained above, they will not try to maintain any particular relationship between their real balances and any other element in their demand for real balances such as the interest rate or their real income. If the government creates money, say, through Federal Reserve purchases of government securities, they will simply accumulate the additional cash balances. If the government destroys money, they will exchange cash for government securities without changing their demands for goods or for other assets. Absolute liquidity preference implies that the quantity theory is empty—that, because the demand for real balances is highly "elastic" with respect to interest rates, velocity (hence, demand) is highly unstable. Because money supply changes generate proportionate changes in velocity in the opposite direction, the quantity of money has no effect on output or prices. Absolute liquidity preference characterizes economic slumps. The deeper the slump, the deeper the "liquidity trap."

During the nineteen-sixties Friedman and Anna J. Schwartz performed a number of studies for the National Bureau of Economic Research (NBER), in which they investigated the relationship between money and cyclical behavior. In one of these studies, they found that, since 1869, the velocity of money in the United States has been "highly stable," exhibiting, for the most part, a gradual decline. "In response to cyclical fluctuations, velocity has shown a systematic and stable movement about its trend, rising during expansion and falling during contraction."[12] In a subsequent study, they compared U.S. money growth rates with turning points in NBER "reference cycles" and found that money growth rates exhibit peak rates of change early in expansion and troughs early in recession. Peaks in money growth rates lead reference cycle peaks by 18 months on the average. Troughs in money growth rates lead reference cycle troughs by 12 months on the average.[13]

Friedman observed that "these regular and sizable leads of the money series are themselves suggestive of an influence running from money to business but they are by no means decisive."[14] Perhaps the influence runs in the other direction, so that business expansion generally causes increases, with a lag, in money growth rates and contraction generally causes decreases, with a lag, in money growth rates. As a test, Friedman compared the dispersion of leads and lags between money growth-rate and reference-cycle peaks and troughs. He found that the dispersion of leads from money-growth-rate peaks and troughs to reference-cycle peaks and troughs has been smaller than the dispersion of lags from reference-cycle peaks and troughs to

---

[12] Milton Friedman and Anna J. Schwartz, *A Monetary History of the United States, 1869–1960* (Princeton, N.J.: Princeton University Press for the National Bureau of Economic Research, 1963). p. 682.

[13] Milton Friedman and Anna J. Schwartz, "Money and Business Cycles," *Review of Economics and Statistics*, 45 (February, 1963), in *The Optimum Quantity of Money and Other Essays*, pp. 194, 196.

[14] Milton Friedman, "The Monetary Studies of the National Bureau," *The National Bureau Enters its 45th Year*, 44th Annual Report, pp. 7-25, in *The Optimum Quantity of Money and Other Essays*, p. 269.

money-growth-rate peaks and troughs, suggesting that the direction of influence is from money to business.

Friedman and Schwartz found that the changes in money income and prices that marked every major episode (deep depression or major inflation) in U.S. economic history were "accompanied by a change in the rate of growth of the money stock, in the same direction and of appreciable magnitude." Inasmuch as this "cannot consistently be explained by the contemporary changes in money income and prices," either it must stem from coincidence or "it must reflect an influence running from money to business."[15] The authors were unable, by way of contrast, to identify as consistent a relationship between investment and the business cycle. Neither investment alone nor "autonomous expenditures" (investment plus government purchases) exhibited a strong positive relationship with economic activity during major episodes.

Friedman and David Meiselman produced evidence that cast doubt both on the importance of investment as a determinant of cyclical behavior and on the stability of the Keynesian multiplier.[16] They found that the correlation between money and income was greater and more stable than the correlation between autonomous expenditures and income.

> These results are striking because they contradict so sharply the widespread presumption among economists that investment (or, more generally, autonomous expenditure) is the prime mover in cyclical fluctuations, transmitting its influence to the rest of income via a multiplier effect on consumption. So far as these results go, they suggest that, *for a given stock of money*, there is no systematic relation at all between autonomous expenditures and consumption — in experience, the multiplier effect on consumption is as likely to be negative as positive.[17]

Friedman's empirical research led him to conclude that money is a stabler and more important determinant of business cycle behavior than autonomous expenditures and that the velocity of money is stabler than the Keynesian multiplier. In that sense, he provided a factual basis for the post-Keynesian slogan that "money matters." As forcefully as he has argued the importance of money in driving cycli-

---

[15] Friedman and Schwartz, "Money and Business Cycles," in *The Optimum Quantity of Money and Other Essays*, p. 216.

[16] Milton Friedman and David Meiselman, "The Relative Stability of Monetary Velocity and the Investment Multiplier in the United States, 1897–1958," in *Stabilization Policies* (Englewood Cliffs, N.J.: Prentice-Hall for the Commission on Money and Credit, 1963), pp. 165–268.

[17] Friedman and Schwartz, "Money and Business Cycles," in *The Optimum Quantity of Money and Other Essays*, p. 212.

cal behavior, however, Friedman has argued against the idea of "discretionary" efforts by the Federal Reserve to smooth out the business cycle through appropriate modification of money-supply growth rates. Repeatedly he has argued that, despite the importance of money-growth-rate changes as a leading indicator, the lags that separate peaks and troughs in money cycles from peaks and troughs in general business cycles are long and variable. As a result Federal Reserve efforts to smooth out business cycles are often self-defeating. Because no Federal Reserve (or any) economist is prescient and because Federal Reserve instruments for controlling money growth rates are not amenable to fine tuning, an expansive monetary policy undertaken now to cure a recession might only exacerbate the inflation to follow. An anti-inflation action taken now might deepen the recession to follow. For these and other reasons, the sensible course for the Federal Reserve is to adopt a monetary rule that would bring the actual money growth rate in line with the rate that would provide for stable prices over the long run. By one calculation, this would be about 4 percent — 3 percent for long-run growth in real output plus 1 percent for long-run decline in velocity.[18]

Whatever the rule, it would, if properly chosen and implemented, perform far better than the rules or lack of rules that governed money supply growth rates in the past. A stable monetary rule would have avoided or at least tempered every major depression — including the Great Depression, during which the money supply fell by one-third — and every major inflationary episode in U.S. history. But in absorbing this lesson, it is important not to overreact against "simple-minded Keynesianism."

Following the war, the United States and other countries found themselves beset by inflation, rather than depression. Keynes was seen as having imparted an inflationary bias to public policy by propagating the argument that full employment requires expansive fiscal measures and that money (often, at least) doesn't matter. By the nineteen-fifties, many economists and public officials had moved to an opposite point of view — that the government should engage in aggressive and discretionary monetary policy to offset swings in the business cycle. It was against this point of view that Friedman urged a monetary rule:

> I stress nonetheless the similarity between the views that prevailed in the late twenties and those that prevail today because I fear that, now as then, the pendulum may have swung too far, that, now as then, we are in danger of assigning to monetary policy a larger role

---
[18]Milton Friedman, *A Program for Monetary Stability* (New York: Fordham University Press, 1959), p. 91.

than it can perform, in danger of asking it to accomplish tasks that it cannot achieve, and, as a result, in danger of preventing it from making the contribution that it is capable of making.[19]

This statement encapsulates monetarist thinking as it had evolved up to the time that other writers, expanding upon a point made by Friedman, began to develop a theory of cyclical behavior based on rational expectations. There are, in this thinking, elements of agreement and potential disagreement with supply side theory. But, for the most part, the monetarists and the supply siders have focused on different issues. The monetarist revolution focused on the stability of money velocity, as compared to the Keynesian multiplier. It challenged and largely discredited Keynes's argument that, because of accommodating changes in velocity, money-supply changes often have no effect on either output or prices. The supply siders have stressed the nonexistence of money illusion, the importance of relative prices, and the link between saving and investment. The point at issue is how strong and reliable an effect money can exert on real output — an effect for which monetarists, but not all supply siders, would allow.

I will use the remainder of this paper to argue that rational expectations offers a reconciliation. That a reconciliation may be timely is suggested by the tenor of recent commentary in the press, wherein some supply siders have been urging confrontation.[20]

Toward Rational Expectations

In his 1848 treatise on *Principles of Political Economy*, John Stuart Mill argued that, in the long run, the quantity of money has no effect on the rate of interest:

> The greater or smaller the number of counters which must be used to express a given amount of real wealth, makes no difference in the position of or interests of lenders or borrowers, and therefore makes no difference in the demand or supply of loans. There is the same amount of real capital lent or borrowed; and if the capital in the hands of lenders is represented by a greater number of pounds sterling, the same greater number of pounds sterling will, in consequence of the rise in prices, be now required for the purposes to which the borrowers intend to apply them.[21]

---

[19] Milton Friedman, "The Role of Monetary Policy," p. 5.

[20] See, for example, Jude Wanniski, "The Burden of Friedman's Monetarism," *New York Times*, July 26, 1981. In a shrill attack the author accuses Friedman of advocating a "managed currency" that would amount to the very fine tuning against which Friedman has always argued.

[21] John Stuart Mill, *Principles of Political Economy* (London: Longmans, Green, and Co., 1923), p. 645.

In the short run, money creation by government will affect the rate of interest, "but in a contrary way to that which is generally supposed; by raising, not by lowering it." The reason is that lenders will expect money creation to lead to higher prices and will adjust the interest rate accordingly: "Lenders who expect that their interest will be paid, and the principal perhaps redeemed, in a less valuable currency than they lent, of course require a rate of interest sufficient to cover this contingent loss."[22]

More recently, but years before Keynes published his *General Theory*, Irving Fisher examined statistically the proposition that the nominal or "money" rate of interest varies directly with the rate of inflation. He found that the correlation between U.S. interest rates and inflation rates is highest when the adjustment of interest rates to inflation is spread over twenty years. In a world of perfect foresight, lenders would adjust the nominal rates of interest that they demand from borrowers continuously and immediately in response to changes in the actual inflation rate. Real interest rates would remain unchanged, but for variations in the productivity of capital and in the urgency that households attach to present consumption. But in the real world, money illusion and other factors get in the way of this process. People do not revise their expectations concerning money's future purchasing power immediately as that purchasing power changes or could be expected to change.[23]

These observations by Mill and Fisher illustrate what may now be the single most important problem in macroeconomics—the role of people's expectations in determining the behavior of nominal and real economic phenomena and the rate at which their expectations adjust to changes in currently available information concerning the behavior of those phenomena. If people act according to "rational expectations," they will adjust their expectations in line with the information that is available to them (or that they find it worthwhile to acquire). Acting as suppliers or demanders of economic resources, they will set their supply or demand prices accordingly. For Mill and Fisher, this meant that inflation will lead to higher nominal interest rates—an issue that goes to the heart of the debate that was to arise later between the Keynesians and the monetarists. More generally, it meant that sooner or later economists would have to come to grips with a number of issues, which, perhaps in part because of the psychological considerations involved, they had previously sloughed over, using terms like "money illusion" that beg the most important questions.

---

[22]*Ibid.*, p. 646.
[23]Irving Fisher, *The Theory of Interest* (New York: Macmillan, 1930), p. 494.

In what Robert Gordon has described as probably "the most influential article written in macroeconomics in the past two decades,"[24] Milton Friedman extended Fisher's framework to the analysis of unemployment. Just as there is some real rate of interest that links the productivity of physical capital to the time preferences of households, there is a natural rate of unemployment that corresponds to the existing level of real wage rates. This is the level of unemployment that would exist if all employers took advantage of all the existing information concerning the level of real wages, given "the actual structural characteristics of the labor and commodity markets, including market imperfections, stochastic variability in demands and supplies, the cost of gathering information about job vacancies and labor availabilities, and so on."[25]

This passage offers an analogy to what Nordic-Americans like to call the "pre-Columbian era of transatlantic exploration." In the supply side framework, there is no involuntary unemployment except insofar as workers are prevented from offering their services at low enough real wage rates to make themselves attractive to prospective employers. Friedman's natural rate of unemployment antedates this interpretation. The natural rate of unemployment (or its supply side obverse, the equilibrium rate of employment) depends on relative prices, as distorted by all those things that get in the way of mutually beneficial exchange—minimum wages, unions, and, Friedman could have added, taxes.

Friedman's argument concerning the natural rate of unemployment antedates present-day supply side thinking, first, by emphasizing the idea that the level of real output depends on relative prices and, second, by allowing for deviations in real output from a natural trend path. Friedman's natural rate of unemployment corresponds closely also to the notion of "normal" or "full information" output that writers in the rational expectations camp were later to adopt.

Friedman argued that, whereas "there is always a temporary trade-off between inflation and unemployment; there is no permanent trade-off." Imagine a graph with the rate of inflation (or, in the Phillips article, rate of change in nominal wages) on the vertical axis and the rate of unemployment on the horizontal axis. Then, Friedman argued, the curve slopes gradually downward in the short run but is vertical in the long run. In the short run, the monetary authorities can always induce a little more production and employment by bringing about a little more inflation. But, in the long run, their ef-

---

[24]Robert J. Gordon, "Output Fluctuations and Gradual Price Adjustment," *Journal of Economic Literature*, XIX (June, 1981), p. 504.

[25]Friedman, "The Role of Monetary Policy," p. 8.

forts will prove futile as the economy gravitates back to its long-run (supply side, one might say) path. The only reason why even short-run real output increases are possible in this way is that workers are capable of being temporarily fooled about the real wage rates they actually face. Suppose employers respond to an unanticipated rise in demand by hiring more workers. This will be just the first step in a process that leads, everything else the same, back to the initial level of output and employment:

> Because selling prices of products typically respond to an unanticipated rise in nominal demand faster than prices of factors of production, real wages received have gone down—though real wages anticipated by employees went up, since employees implicitly evaluated the wages offered at the earlier price level. Indeed, the simultaneous fall *ex post* in real wages to employers and rise *ex ante* in real wages to employees is what enabled employment to increase. But the decline *ex post* in real wages will soon come to affect anticipations. Employees will start to reckon on rising prices of the things they buy and to demand higher nominal wages for the future. "Market" unemployment is below the "natural" level. There is an excess demand for labor so real wages will tend to rise toward their initial level.[26]

While this analysis clearly justified Gordon's flattering evaluation, both as an interpretation of stagflation and as a precursor of present-day thinking, it leaves much unexplained. Why should it take workers more time to figure out that the prices of goods have risen than to figure out that their nominal wage rates have risen? Both go up simultaneously in response to an unanticipated demand increase. In turn, then, as supply siders might ask, why should there by any real output effect stemming from a demand "surprise"? Friedman cited evidence that the initial real output effects last two to five years and that the full effects are not fully dissipated for twenty years.[27] But why such long lags? Friedman based his argument in part on the assumption that workers expect prices to be stable because prices have been stable in the past and because "prices and wages have been set for some time in the future on that basis."[28] Yet, as events were beginning to prove at the time he was making this argument, prices and wages can rise at higher and higher rates without noticeable gains in employment.

Two pieces of information appeared to be missing. First, what determines people's expectations of current or future economic events and second, how fast do they revise their expectations in the light of

---
[26]*Ibid.*, p. 10.
[27]*Ibid.*, p. 11.
[28]*Ibid.*, p. 10.

new information concerning the likely course of those events? Taken together, these pieces of information would determine the magnitude and the duration of any effects that demand surprises might have on relative prices and therefore real output.

In a later article, Friedman laid out a common model that encapsulated the fundamental workings of the quantity theory and the (Keynesian) income expenditure theory. As such, however, the model was incomplete: there were only five equations for six unknowns. In order to complete the model and, thereby, to solve for the six unknowns the model is purported to explain, it was necessary to provide the "missing equation." This could be one of two equations: a "simple quantity theory" equation that determined the level of real income or a "simple expenditure theory" equation that determined the level of prices. Both were determined "outside the system."[29]

The "missing equation" epitomizes the dialectic into which present day macroeconomics has evolved. Friedman found it possible to organize the major ideas of both the modern quantity theorists and of Keynes into a single model that was complete but for a separate theory of real output or prices. The missing equation would explain in part how people's expectations and, therefore, their perceptions concerning relative prices adjust to demand surprises attributable to changes in monetary policy. It is to the efforts of writers in the rational expectations school to remedy this deficiency that we now turn.

Phelpsian Islands and Lucas Supply Curves

In his introduction to a volume on *Microeconomic Foundations of Employment and Inflation Theory*, Edmund S. Phelps postulated an economy made up of islands separated from each other by one day's travel. Producers are in pure competition in interisland as well as intraisland trade, meaning that there are so many producers that none can influence the prices at which he sells goods or hires labor. Workers know without cost the real wages they can obtain on their respective islands but find that they can determine the real wages that prevail on a neighboring island only by giving up a day's work and visiting the island to sample nominal wage rates there.

Demand surprises, in this scenario, can lead to changes in real employment without workers' suffering any form of money illusion. Workers suffer, instead, from a lack of perfect information that causes them occasionally to confuse general price changes with relative price changes. Suppose, following Phelps, that real wages are

---

[29]Milton Friedman, "A Theoretical Framework for Monetary Analysis," *Journal of Political Economy*, 78 (March/April, 1970), pp. 193–238.

temporarily the same on all islands. Then, there is a general decline in demand, causing prices and nominal wage rates to fall proportionately and by the same amounts on all islands. Separated as they are from other islands, workers on a given island will not automatically infer that real wages are unchanged throughout the island economy. They will, instead, attribute at least part of the local decline in demand to local conditions only. They will give up some work time on the home island to visit other islands on the expectation that nominal wages there have held up better than at home. Hours worked in all islands will fall and remain depressed until workers have verified that the decline in nominal wage rates is economy wide in scope.[30]

Phelps' model generates real output effects by inducing workers to perform tradeoffs between work time and search time. Suppose, in his scenario, that there is only one homogeneous good, so that workers find it easy to determine the overall price level. Knowing that there is pure competition between producers, they will know that the price of the one good produced throughout the interisland economy will be everywhere the same and will move everywhere in tandem. Nominal wages are another matter, however, separated as workers are from one another. Workers on a given island know that nominal wages there need not always equal nominal wages elsewhere, owing to imperfections in information about labor market opportunities elsewhere. Suppose, to carry the example further, the single good that workers produce is oil. Pure competition keeps the price of oil everywhere the same, but not the price of labor. The discovery of a rich oil field on one island will allow producers there to profit by hiring labor from neighboring islands. Workers on neighboring islands that have relatively poor oil fields will see their own wages fall as the interisland supply of oil increases. But they will not know whether the reason lies in general or local conditions. The reason could be general, say, owing to a decision by the interisland central bank to reduce the money supply. Or it could be local, owing to a decline in the relative profitability of local oil fields. Only by engaging in routine examinations of the nominal wages paid on other islands can they know for sure. Thus, if the central bank happens to reduce the money supply unexpectedly, it can bring about losses in real output by inducing workers to substitute additional search time for work time. Alternatively, it can bring about temporary increases in real output by increasing the money supply and fooling workers

---

[30]Edmund S. Phelps, "Introduction: The New Microeconomics in Employment and Inflation Theory," *Microeconomic Foundations of Employment and Inflation Theory* (New York: W. W. Norton & Company, Inc., 1970), pp. 6–7.

into giving up some of their routine search time in exchange for what appear to be higher nominal wage opportunities at home.

In a later series of articles, Robert E. Lucas developed a formal theory of supply based on the methods used by economic agents to distinguish relative from absolute price changes. In Lucas's framework the supply of goods has a "normal" and a cyclical component. The normal component behaves according to Friedman's natural rate hypothesis, varying only with the "real" conditions that underlie household supply and demand. The cyclical component varies with deviations between the prices that prevail in individual markets and with what producers perceive to be the current general price level.

Let us suppose, following Lucas, that a producer will set actual output equal to normal output if the actual price he is offered for his goods equals what he believes to be the prevailing general price of goods. On the other hand, the producer, knowing that information concerning the prices of goods is imperfect, will offer more than the normal amount for sale if he determines that the price he is offered exceeds the general price level and less than that amount if he determines that the price he is offered is less than the general price level.

What causes cyclical behavior in this model is uncertainty about the actual size of the general price level. Each producer formulates his determination (or "expectation") about the size of the general price level in a given production period from two pieces of information: (1) observations on what the general price level has been in past production periods and (2) his knowledge of the way in which individual market prices tend to distribute themselves around the general price level. From his observations of the general price level over past production periods, he computes an average, historical general price level and formulates a distribution of those observations around the average. This gives him one more piece of information — the dispersion (or "variance") of the general price level around its historical average — which he can combine with knowledge of the dispersion of existing market prices around the general price level to determine his own best estimate of the actual, current general price level. This estimate is a weighted average sum of the price he faces in his own market and the average, historical general price level. The weight that the producer attaches to his own market price in computing this average is greater, the smaller the known dispersion in individual market prices relative to the known dispersion in the general price level. The weight that he attaches to the average general price level is greater, the greater the known dispersion in individual market prices relative to the known dispersion in the general price level. Hence, if the general price level has been "stable" over the past, so that its known dispersion is small, the individual producer will interpret a change in the price he faces as a change in the price he faces relative to the general price level. He will attach a small weight to his own market price and a large weight to the average, historical general price level in computing what he determines to be the existing general price level.

If, for example, the monetary authorities interrupt a long period of stable money and stable prices with an unexpected increase in the money supply, individual producers will falsely interpret the resulting rise in the general price level as consisting mainly of a rise in current market prices they face relative to the general price level. (This is because they give so high a weight to the average, historical general price level in assessing the current period general price level.) They will respond by producing more goods and will continue to produce more goods until they have revised their calculation of the general price level and of the dispersion of the general price level around its average.[31]

Lucas's model can be applied to Friedman's explanation, above, of how actual employment can deviate temporarily from the "natural rate" level of employment. Suppose now that workers, following the example set by producers in Lucas's model, use information on historical prices and nominal wages to determine the average, historical general price level (we may call this the average, historical consumer price index or CPI) and its dispersion and the average, historical nominal wage rate and its dispersion. Suppose also that both indicators have been stable, so that their dispersion around the average is small. We allow that a worker buys more than one good but assume that he limits his purchases of goods and his offers of work time to particular markets. These markets may have different geographical characteristics and may embody different combinations of goods or places of work.

Now a demand surprise brought about by money creation will cause the prices offered producers for goods to rise as consumers try to bid goods away from each other. Producers will, in turn, find that they can profitably eke out more production by raising nominal wage rates. As long as producers bid up nominal wages less rapidly than consumers bid up prices (as long as real wages fall), producers can increase profits by hiring more labor and producing more goods.

Lucas provides an answer to the question why workers would be willing to offer more work time in this setting, despite falling real wages. The answer is that workers would evaluate both the rise in prices that they face as consumers and the rise in nominal wage rates

---

[31]Robert E. Lucas, "Some International Evidence on Output-Inflation Tradeoffs," *American Economic Review*, 63 (June, 1973), pp. 326–334.

that they are offered as workers to be "local" phenomena and hence mainly indicative of relative price changes. Because the CPI has been "stable," the individual worker would interpret the higher prices paid by him for goods as localized to the market in which he traditionally buys them. He would perceive the rise in prices of goods in that market as meaning that the prices of goods in that market have increased relative to the prices of goods in other markets. Likewise, because nominal wage rates have been stable, he would perceive the employer as offering him a higher nominal wage rate than he would command elsewhere. He would thereupon offer more labor to his current employer and switch his purchases of goods to other markets. Only when he determines that the rise in prices and in nominal wage rates had been general in scope would he revert to his earlier level of work effort and, possibly, his earlier shopping patterns.

Equations that relate real output to differences between actual market prices and expected market prices are now known as Lucas supply curves. A Lucas supply curve provides an analytical framework within which it is possible to observe and measure people's perceptions of current economic events. As formulated by Lucas, this supply curve relates current output to the differences between the individual market prices that exist now and people's expectations concerning the current general price level. Thomas Sargent and Neil Wallace have offered an alternative formulation in which output varies with the difference between the actual current general price level and the general price level that people expected, in the last production period, to prevail during this production period.[32]

Numerous objections can be raised concerning the rarified atmosphere in which the participants in the original Phelpsian scenario or in Lucas's more formalistic model are forced to act out their lives. Why, it may be asked, don't Phelps' workers merely hire a survey research firm to submit regular reports on interisland wage rates? Why don't workers in the extension of Lucas's model, above, merely wait until the next CPI is published before jumping to the conclusion that the higher consumer prices they face are an isolated phenomenon? The answer is that, in these examples, as in real life, surveys and price indexes are themselves only imperfect representations of what they purport to measure. Suppose the producer with the rich oil field falls outside the sample of surveyed employers. Suppose that workers regard the CPI as only a partially reliable index of the general price level. Then workers in both scenarios will find it rational

---

[32] Thomas J. Sargent and Neil Wallace, " 'Rational' Expectations, the Optimal Monetary Instrument, and the Optimal Money Supply Rate," *Journal of Political Economy*, 83 (April, 1975), pp. 242–243.

not to rely on published data for forming their expectations concerning absolute prices. They will wish to draw, in addition, on individual search and experimentation, both of which tend to impart different perceptions to different persons. While this may complicate the job of modeling and forecasting the aggregate response to demand surprises, it does not vitiate the conclusion that the response may have real as well as nominal dimensions.

The rational expectations framework should not be thought to provide an exhaustive accounting of the real output effects that may be brought about by changes in money-supply growth rates. The contributions by Lucas, Sargent, and Wallace in the early seventies provided a theoretical link between real output and demand surprises, which in the monetarist framework, originate from money-supply surprises. Now a second generation of writers is finding that even anticipated money-supply changes can exert real output effects when the rational expectations paradigm is extended to the behavior of inventories.[33]

Wherever this research finally leads, the early writers in the rational expectations field have made one accomplishment of great current practical value: they have provided the required missing link between the analysis of supply side effects and the analysis of money-supply effects stemming from government policy changes. The rational expectations models rest on all the assumptions that underly supply side thinking but one. People act in their self interest, markets clear (there is no persistent, "involuntary" unemployment), people act on the basis of the best information available to them, and real output depends on perceived variations in relative prices. The one difference is that perceived relative prices do not necessarily equal actual relative prices. Rational expectations takes into consideration the fact that information is scarce and that, in the real world, people do not adapt their expectations to prevailing economic policies and conditions with textbook precision. Below we observe that the imprecision with which people adapt their expectations to policy changes may stem in part from their unwillingness to place confidence in government's willingness to adhere to a rational policy line. This poses a problem for the success of economic policy irrespective of its theoretical underpinnings.

There is no money illusion in the rational expectations framework. Workers do not offer more work time following an unanticipated spurt of monetary growth because they feel better off with higher nominal wage rates but lower real wage rates. Rather, they

---

[33] See, for example, Alan S. Blinder, "Inventories and the Structure of Macro Models," *American Economic Review*, 71 (May, 1981), pp. 11–16.

offer more work time because they perceive, using the best information available to them, that their real wage rates have risen.

Rational expectations offers, in a sense, the minimum concession that supply siders can offer to the existence of a link between money supply and real output changes. Indeed the rational expectations paradigm is itself vulnerable for having reduced the role of money in determining cyclical behavior to the error term in a regression equation. Franco Modigliani derides Thomas Sargent's macroeconomic model for implying that "what happened in the 1930's was a severe attack of contagious laziness."[34]

The contribution made by Sargent and the other writers surveyed here is that they have punctured the Keynesian myth of contagious irrationality—of workers knowingly foregoing laziness in exchange for lower real wage rates. The rational expectations school explains that there is a difference between rational and "adaptive" expectations—that workers and lenders are as good as economists at figuring out that a spurt in monetary growth is likely to generate inflation, irrespective of past price behavior. Models that are "autoregressive" or "extrapolative" in character—that have people formulate their expectations concerning future price changes according to past price changes only—are misspecified and tend to exaggerate the lags with which people bring their expectations into line with reality.[35]

The empirical studies of Friedman and Schwartz did not decompose the effects of money growth rate changes into their real and nominal components or identify the link between the formulation of people's expectations and the dissipation of real effects. In an effort to fill this gap, Leonall Andersen and Denis Karnosky examined the relationship between percentage changes in the money supply and percentage changes in prices and in real output. They found that permanent changes in monetary growth tend to be followed by "a sharp and substantial positive response of output growth for five quarters," whereas it takes the rate of price inflation at least 20 quarters to adjust.[36]

In a later study, John Rutledge examined the effects of changes in the growth of money—separated into anticipated and unanticipated components—on prices and real output. He found that the adjustment of real output to an unanticipated change in the growth of

---

[34]Franco Modigliani, "The Monetarist Controversy or, Should We Forsake Stabilization Policies?" *American Economic Review*, 67 (March, 1977), p. 6.

[35]See John Rutledge, *A Monetarist Model of Inflationary Expectations* (Lexington, Massachusetts: D. C. Heath, 1974), pp. 7–27.

[36]Leonall C. Andersen and Denis S. Karnosky, "The Appropriate Time Frame for Controlling Monetary Aggregates: The St. Louis Evidence," in *Controlling Monetary Aggregates II: The Implementation* (Boston: Federal Reserve Bank of Boston, 1973), pp. 147–177.

money is about the same as the adjustment of prices to an anticipated change in the growth of money. Both take about eleven quarters to work themselves out.[37] Robert Barro has estimated that an unanticipated rise of one percent in the growth of money will generate, in the same year, about a .36 percent rise in the price level and almost a one percent rise in real output. The price effect and the real output effect take, respectively, five years and two years to work themselves out.[38]

All such estimates may be—and have been—criticized as mere statistical exercises.[39] While they may reveal an association between money, prices, and real output, that association could be purely coincidental. A truly convincing demonstration would derive the purported effects of money growth changes from a model of producer or worker behavior such as we explored above. Such a model would explain how people adjust their expectations to policy changes and other changes. But even without a demonstration of this kind, it appears that policy makers should recognize the existence of real output effects attributable to monetary surprises. What remains to be determined is how quickly people adjust their expectations to changes in government policy when the only policy surprise may be a return to a rational policy line.

Beyond Rational Expectations

Commenting on the failures of macroeconomic stabilization policies during the seventies, William Fellner has observed that "the difficulties of enforcing a price level target through demand management policy come mainly from the fact that in the given Western institutional setting the public's attitude toward policy has become one of self-justifying skepticism."[40] It is the failure of governments to develop and maintain an identifiable system of some kind for managing aggregate demand that makes it impossible for government to forecast the effects of its actions on people's expectations or, therefore, on prices and outputs.

Rational expectations, says Fellner, reduces to two central propositions: (1) that the systematic or anticipated components of government demand-management policy will be neutral with respect to real economic variables and (2) that demand management policies aimed

---

[37]John Rutledge, "The Effect of Money on Prices," in *Third West Coast Academic/Federal Reserve Seminar* (San Francisco: Federal Reserve Bank of San Francisco, 1980), pp. 120-127.

[38]Robert J. Barro, "Unanticipated Money and Economic Activity: Results from Annual U.S. Data," in *Rational Expectations and Economic Policy*, ed. by Stanley Fischer (Chicago: University of Chicago Press, 1980), pp. 23-24.

[39]See comments on Barro's paper, *ibid.*, pp. 49-72.

[40]William Fellner, *Towards a Reconstruction of Macroeconomics* (Washington, D.C.: American Enterprise Institute for Public Policy Research, 1976), p. 116.

at influencing those variables will, therefore, be ineffective.[41] While failure by government to develop and maintain a credible policy line will tend, if anything, to make the second proposition more applicable, it will also tend to deprive the first of its meaning. In order for the monetary arm of government to predict with some success that the anticipated components of its policy actions will affect only prices and not output, it must be possible to figure out in the first place what those components are. The less consistent a policy the monetary authorities have followed in the past, the more consistently they will have to behave in the future in order to establish credibility.

This line of reasoning represents what may be the principal challenge to the Reagan Administration's New Beginning. The rapid move by the Administration to reduce tax rates and to bring monetary growth under control represents a determined and highly visible effort to reverse the earlier drift of economic policy and to establish a credible policy line. As part of that effort, the Administration has begun to incorporate in its forecasts of economic activity some of the tenets of rational expectations theory, including the idea that people formulate their expectations of future price changes according to what they expect policy to be in the future and not just according to what they have observed policy to be in the past. The difficulty is that the Administration has inherited a state of affairs from which it is difficult to infer any line of policy. As a result, the application of rational expectations to the analysis of current policy effects may be premature and may tend to exaggerate the speed with which price stability can be restored and to understate the temporary, adverse consequences for real economic activity of restoring price stability. Supply side economics and rational expectations are properly matched, but only in the context of cautious optimism concerning the ability of government to bring about a state of affairs in which their teachings can be made operational.

---

[41]William Fellner, "The Valid Core of Rationality Hypothesis in the Theory of Expectations," *Journal of Money, Credit and Banking*, XII (November, 1980, Part 2), p. 768.

THE ENTERPRISE SYSTEM, DEMOCRACY, AND THE GENERAL WELFARE: AN APPROACH TO RECONCILIATION

by

RICHARD E. WAGNER

Richard E. Wagner is a Professor of Economics and Policy Sciences at Florida State University and is a contributing author to the American Enterprise Institute.

DEMOCRACY AND A MARKET ECONOMY ARE COMMONLY thought to complement one another, with each being a necessary facet of a society premised on the liberal value system which characterizes American society. It is easy to see why this complementarity is thought to exist. In a market economy, entrepreneurs make the initial choices of what to produce, but consumers are free to accept or reject those choices. This freedom of consumer choice in the presence of competition among entrepreneurs brings about the actual sovereignty of consumers over what is produced. In a democracy, political entrepreneurs (politicians) similarly make the initial choices of what programs and policies to offer to the public, but citizens are able to register their approval or disapproval at the ballot box, as well as in other ways. Moreover, incumbent politicians are not monopolists; there is competition in politics just as there is in business, and this competition, it is suggested, ensures that it is the citizens who are actually sovereign over political outcomes. Hence, the sovereignty of consumers within the market economy combines with the sovereignty of citizens within the polity, with each system thereby complementing the other in the institutional order of a liberal or free society.

While this portrait of a congruence between democracy and a market economy is comforting, much reason and experience suggests that any such congruence is not a necessary feature of social life, but rather is a product of a proper institutional order. Students of political theory and history have long noted that while democracy may support the liberty and the prosperity of those who live within its boundaries, it also contains a latent tendency to replace the promotion of the common interest in liberty and prosperity with the promotion of particularized interests. To the extent this happens, a politics of wealth creation is replaced by a politics of wealth transfer, and wealth erosion. Wealth can be transferred, moreover, only through restrictions on liberty. Wealth cannot, for instance, be transferred to tenants through rent control without eroding the liberty of the owner of the rental property; wealth cannot be transferred to unionized garment workers without proscribing the liberty of people to make in their own homes garments for resale. A politics in which members of a ruling majority coalition transfer wealth to themselves from the remainder of society not only destroys wealth through the disincentive effects that arise, but also it reduces concomitantly the extent of liberty.

In recent years there have emerged several expressions of concern about the curtailment of liberty and the erosion of prosperity that have come about through the workings of contemporary democracy. A variety of state and local governments have placed limits on taxes and expenditures. Substantial efforts to place constraints on the budgetary adventures of the federal government have been making progress, as reflected most recently perhaps by the Judiciary Committee of the U.S. Senate reporting out by an 11 to 5 vote a proposal to limit the rate of growth of the federal budget. And deregulation has captured considerable interest. The extent to which such efforts as these will be successful in constraining the wealth eroding properties of contemporary democracy is an open question. What is perhaps of greatest importance is simply to note that these efforts represent a growing recognition of the tendencies toward wealth transfers and destruction, as against wealth creation, within contemporary democracy, along with some groping for a means of placing firmer control over those tendencies.

The danger to prosperity and liberty that results from the tax-transfer politics that has proliferated in contemporary democracy is what James Madison described as the "violence of faction" in his famous essay, *Federalist* No. 10. As Madison noted there, "By a faction I understand a number of citizens, whether amounting to a majority or minority of the whole, who are united and actuated by some common impulse of passion, or of interest, adverse to the rights of other citizens, or to the permanent and aggregate interests of the community." Faction refers, among other things, to the ability of the members of a winning coalition to enrich themselves at the expense of the remainder of society. In a market system, people enrich themselves by providing services that are valued by others, so the market system is wealth enhancing for society. Madison recognized that it was possible for a system of democracy to operate similarly, but he also recognized that it was by no means necessary that it operate in such a wealth enhancing fashion. Democracy could act in this manner only as the problem of faction or tax-transfer politics was overcome, which in turn, was a problem of the appropriate form of democracy. Democracy and the market economy are not inherently reconciled with the general welfare; the lesson Madison had learned so well was that reconciliation was a matter of the proper form of democracy, and the authors of the *Federalist Papers* went on to describe what this might involve for their world of the late 18th century.

The purpose of this essay is to explore, in light of some recently developing scholarship on the interaction between politics and economics, the consequences of Madison's insight for contemporary democracy, and for the requisites for any reconciliation of democracy, the enterprise system, and the general welfare. At base, this essay argues that the reason why a market economy is a wealth enhancing rather than a wealth eroding system is that its institutional framework of ownership and contract actually promotes consensus as to the values of different patterns of resource usage. Without such a consensual orientation, wealth enhancement would lose its dominance. In like manner, democracy can be said to be wealth enhancing rather than wealth eroding to the extent its institutions are consensual rather than majoritarian in their operation. In other words, there are many particular institutional orders consistent with the general idea of democracy, and wealth enhancement will come to dominate wealth erosion to the extent that the particular institutions of democracy come to reflect in one way or another the features of ownership and contract.

Scarcity and the Problem of Economic Calculation in Society

Economic and political activity both arise because societies confront scarcity. The resources available to a society along with the knowledge about how those resources can be used to satisfy wants is insufficient to satisfy all of the wants of all members of society. Accordingly, societies must in one way or another deal with scarcity by making choices about which wants to satisfy and which to leave unsatisfied. A liberal or free society is one in which resources are directed to those uses valued more highly by the members of society, rather than those uses valued most highly by some ruling person, clique, or elite. A market economy is a form of economic organization in which decisions about which wants to satisfy reflect the valuations of the various members of society, as these are indicated by the willingness of different people to pay for the resources they wish to use. A market economy is the way a liberal society, grounded in individual autonomy, addresses its economic questions.

How can it be determined whether a particular use of resources will shift resources from the satisfaction of less valued wants to the satisfaction of more valued wants? For instance, on what basis can a judgment be reached as to whether a proposal to use resources for growing bananas in North Dakota or for turning Atlanta into a port for ocean-going vessels will represent a shift of resources from less valued to more valued uses? This question of economic calculation—

the determination of the value to the individual members who constitute a society of alternative patterns of resource utilization—is the focal point of a famous controversy in economics that raged in the 1920s and 1930s. The particular topic of controversy was how the structure of production in a socialist economy can reflect the valuations of the members of that society. While socialism was initially thought of as replacing a market economy with a planned economy, the outcome of this controversy was recognition that it is impossible for a planned economy to reflect the valuations of the members of society. It might reflect the valuations of a set of planners or rulers, but it cannot reflect the valuations of the members of society. Individual valuations can be reflected in economic outcomes only within an institutional order in which consumers are free to accept or reject the offerings of producers, and in which producers thrive only to the extent they are successful in producing what consumers want. In other words, the existence of an institutional order characterized by ownership and contract are essential requisites for economic calculation.

One person might own land in North Dakota, another might own unassembled greenhouses, and a third might own young banana plants. An entrepreneur will assemble the resources necessary to grow bananas in North Dakota if he thinks the value of the resources when assembled in that form will exceed their value in the forms they could otherwise take. Since choices concerning the utilization of resources take place within the constraints of property and contract, an entrepreneur's ability to assemble resources in a particular manner means that there is actually a social consensus that the entrepreneur's proposal for resource utilization seems to represent a more highly valued use of those resources than some other use. For instance, the land in North Dakota can be used for several purposes besides growing bananas. If the entrepreneur who wishes to grow bananas is able to outbid others, who may wish to grow wheat, this means that the value of the bananas he anticipates the land to yield exceeds the value of the wheat the others anticipate that land to yield. Within the framework of property and contract, there is actually a consensus that resources are utilized in their most highly valued manner. Suppose one person thinks a plot of land will be worth $20,000 for growing bananas. If another person thinks it will be worth $40,000 for growing wheat, he will be the higher bidder for land. And the advocate of growing bananas will tacitly agree that growing wheat is a more valuable use of the land, for to disagree implies that he thinks the land will be worth more than $40,000 for growing bananas, in which event he will be the higher bidder for the land. Regardless of the actual outcome, then, property and contract operate to create a consensus as to which of several possible uses of resources is most valuable, and it is this consensus that makes possible the shifting of resources from less valued to more valued uses.

In a market economy, entrepreneurs initiate decisions to produce, and they necessarily must do so before they can know the true evaluations that consumers place upon those decisions, because those evaluations will be revealed only as consumers make their purchases. If entrepreneurs are correct in their judgment about resource utilization, they will profit, and consumers will gain as well by a structure of production that reflects more accurately their wants. Entrepreneurs may, of course, be incorrect in their judgment that a particular pattern of resource utilization is value enhancing. If so, they will make losses, and consumers will also lose because resources will have been devoted to less valued uses. There is, of course, no guarantee that a particular decision concerning resource utilization will turn out after the fact to have been value enhancing, i.e., profitable, but what can be said is that the system of profit-and-loss, which is implied by property and contract, creates incentives to act prudently. That is, the market economy creates knowledge through people's buying choices about the evaluation of entrepreneurial choices concerning resource utilization, and at the same time it creates an incentive for entrepreneurs to act on that knowledge by seeking to avoid the commitment of resources to uses consumers will not support.

But what if an entrepreneur is able to coerce contributions from other members of society to support his decisions, and, moreover, is able to coerce further contributions to cover any losses that might result because people will not willingly pay enough to cover the cost of the resources he has assembled, whether those resources have taken the form of bananas grown in North Dakota, ocean shipping in Atlanta, or anything else. It can no longer be said that the choice of an entrepreneur to assemble resources and direct them to a particular use represents, before the fact, a consensual presumption that the proposed use of resources is value enhancing. Nor can it be said that the entrepreneur's satisfaction with the outcome after the fact indicates that the usage of resources was indeed value enhancing. It is certainly the case that if those who make decisions concerning the utilization of resources can place the burdens of their mistaken judgments that a particular usage was value enhancing—which can be affirmed only through peoples' choices within a regime of property and contract—upon others, less care will be taken in making choices regarding the use of resources.

Government and the Mixed Economy:
An Approach to Rationalization

The function of government in a liberal society is to reflect and support the values of its individual members. While economic activity is organized predominately through markets, exclusive reliance on markets would result in a variety of failures to use resources in their most valued uses. To avoid such wastage requires proper, and some argue extensive government participation in the economy, with the resulting system of economic order often being called a "mixed economy." The problem of securing the proper organization of this mixed economy is seen as one of achieving the proper blend of private and government participation in different aspects of economic life. Government in a liberal society supports individual values in a number of ways. It does this by promoting internal and external peace, as through the provision of police, courts, and the military. It also does this by providing those goods and services valued by the members of society, but which for one of several possible reasons cannot be provided effectively through ordinary market transactions; these goods and services are commonly called public goods. And it does this by mitigating conflicts among resource uses which would otherwise result in a failure of resources to be used in their most valued employments.

The incompleteness or nonexistence of ownership is a primary reason why resources may not be utilized in their most valuable manner. By now, several illustrations have emerged as paradigmatic in the literature about externalities. A long-standing, well-used example is a factory that emits smoke and soot as a by-product of its production. If the factory is able to avoid responsibility for the increased expenses for painting and laundering it imposes on those who reside in its vicinity, the output of the factory will be excessive, in that the value of the additional output will be less than the damage done to adjacent property. If the factory were responsible for the damage done by its smoke and soot, its product would become more expensive, and so its output would be less. Externalities can also be positive, as when a beekeeper's bees fly into a neighboring orchard and pollinate the apple blossoms there. In this case it is commonly argued that the beekeeper will raise too few bees because he does not take into account the added value of the orchard that results from his decision to keep more bees.

It is sometimes suggested that in the presence of externalities, government must act to correct the market failures that will otherwise result. By taking such corrective action government will be acting as a positive-sum participant in the economic process. In terms of the preceding examples, government will in some manner reduce the amount of smoke and soot emitted by the factory and increase the number of bees kept by the beekeeper. A simple way of doing this is to tax those activities that create negative externalities and to subsidize those that create positive externalities. While there are many complexities surrounding such a simple-sounding prescription, the essential idea is the simple one of taxing that of which less is desired and subsidizing that of which more is desired.

Many of the common illustrations of externalities are, however, inapt because they do not show what they purport to show. If the orchard owner thinks he will gain by the presence of more bees, he can contract with the beekeeper to supply more bees. (Alternatively, the orchard owner could raise his own bees.) So long as the value to the orchard owner that is yielded by the additional bees exceeds the cost of those bees to the beekeeper, it will be possible for both parties to reach an agreement that will leave each of them better off, and such an agreement will remove any possible divergence between individual interest and social interest. And it is essentially the same with the smoke and soot. In principle, those who bear the external costs of the smoke and soot could contract with the factory over a reduction in its emissions of smoke and soot. So long as the damage done by the smoke and soot exceeds the cost to the factory of using either a method of production or a scale of output that entails a lower emission of smoke and soot, some such agreement will be possible. If the factory has the right to use the air as it chooses, it will be worthwhile to those harmed by the smoke and soot to buy the factory's agreement to emit less smoke and soot. Alternatively, if people have some right to clean air, the factory will not be able to purchase the consent of the owners to emit the initial amounts of smoke and soot. Regardless of whether the factory has the right to use the air as it chooses or whether the right to air resides with the adjoining property owners, the same outcome will result, namely, the use of the air in its most highly valued manner, so long as the right of ownership of air is transferable from one person to another.

As a point of departure, the existence of some pattern of transferable ownership is generally of greater significance for avoiding resource wastage than is the particular identity of who owns what.[1] It is the presence of transferable ownership per se that leads to resources being used in their most valuable employments in a society; it is the existence of ownership rights over bees and apple orchards that leads to an employment of bees and trees in such a way as to maximize the combined value of honey and apples. With common ownership of one or the other resource, there will exist a much weakened incentive on the part of any of the members of society to

---

[1] This point has come to be called the Coase Theorem, after Ronald H. Coase, "The Problem of Social Cost," *Journal of Law and Economics*, 3 (October 1960), pp. 1–44. For an important precursory work, see Frank H. Knight, "Some Fallacies in the Interpretation of Social Cost," *Quarterly Journal of Economics*, 38 (August 1924), pp. 582–606.

try to bring about such an outcome. With common ownership, for instance, someone who might see an opportunity for increasing the yield of apples or honey will have little incentive to act upon this belief because most of any resulting increase in value will accrue to others.

It should be apparent by now that externalities arise because of the presence of elements of common ownership. It might generally be thought that the example of the factory and the adjacent owners of property illustrates a problem of externality, while the example of the beekeeper and the apple grower does not. Actually, both cases are formally identical: an action taken by A has the ability to change the value of the resources owned by B. What differs between the two cases is only the extent to which ownership is transferable. With respect to the beekeeper and the apple grower, ownership rights are clearly established and easily transferable. In such a situation it will be in the interest of both parties to make an agreement that places resources in their most highly valued uses. With respect to the factory and the adjacent residents, however, ownership rights are generally indefinite and nontransferable. It is generally impossible for people to buy and sell rights to the use of air. Hence, there is no necessity that the pursuit of individual interest will promote the use of resources in their most highly valued employments.

The establishment of ownership, then, is one way of eliminating problems associated with externalities; by doing this, a reduced role for government in the economy need not interfere with the proper use of government to promote the use of resources in higher valued rather than lower valued uses. However, such an establishment of ownership will not always obviate the difficulties of market failure, because in some instances it may be exceedingly difficult if not impossible to establish such ownership. For instance, the widely dispersed sufferers of the smoke and soot damage from the factory may face insuperable organizational costs if they tried to organize to purchase the agreement of the factory to reduce its emissions. The cost of defining and enforcing a system of ownership can be so high that some system of administrative control might be more effective than reliance upon contractual arrangements.

Besides externalities, it is often suggested that there are many things that cannot be provided effectively through markets, and so must be provided by government if resources are to be devoted to the provision of more valued over less valued wants. Such things are called public goods, and these are contrasted with private goods according to the ease with which it is presumed that they can be provided through market processes of contract and exchange. There are some things for which market provision would seem to work poorly, primarily because it would be difficult if not impossible to make and enforce the needed contractual arrangements. Market failure would thus result, and government could act as a positive-sum participant in the economic process to the extent that it succeeds in overcoming such market failure. The provision of a lighthouse has long served as an illustration of how markets may fail when it comes to the provision of public goods. Once a lighthouse has been provided, its protective beam is available to all ships passing by. Regardless of whether a particular ship makes a payment for using the beam, it is able to receive the service offered by the beam. If it is difficult or impossible to exclude non-payers from using the beam, individual shipowners will be motivated to refrain from offering a payment. The social impact of such individual free riding will be the non-provision, or the underprovision, of the lighthouse, even though all shippers would potentially be better off with its provision.

The role of government in this case is, it is commonly argued, to provide such goods. Through its power to tax, government can compel payments that can be used to provide the lighthouse. If the contractual payments of the marketplace cannot be relied upon to organize the provision of lighthouses, compulsory tax extractions can be used to make their provision possible. The same statement could, of course, be made about such things as movies and concerts, or anything else, for that matter, and yet these things are in fact provided through market arrangements. If it were impossible to exclude non-payers from watching a movie or a concert, people would tend not to pay, with the result being that such things would not be provided, unless they were financed by taxation. Movies and concerts are, of course, financed by payments made by users. The owner of a theater has the right to exclude non-payers, so no problem of free riding arises. With respect to the lighthouses in Great Britain, ships that sailed in the vicinity of a lighthouse were charged for the lighthouse's service upon their arrival in port. While the lighthouse has long served as an archtypical example of a public good, the contractual provision of lighthouses is also an historical fact.[2] It seems indisputable that it is more difficult to monitor a ship's use of a lighthouse beam than it is to monitor a person's use of a theater. Yet such monitoring of lighthouse usage clearly has precedent. There are, of course, cases where such monitoring would be exceedingly difficult and costly at best, if not totally impossible, in which event it becomes impossible for economic activity to become organized through contract and exchange. A variety of illustrations have been advanced as requiring govern-

---

[2] The contractual provision of lighthouses is examined in Ronald H. Coase, "The Lighthouse in Economics," *Journal of Law and Economics*, 17 (October 1974), pp. 357–76.

mental provision, with national defense, basic research, and public health being among the more prominently used illustrations. In such instances as these, government provision can become a way of negating the market failure that would otherwise result because of the impossibility of organizing such activity through contract and exchange.

An Incongruity Between Rationalization and Reality?

To the extent it is difficult if not impossible to exclude those who do not pay for some good or service from using it anyway, the structure of production in an economy organized by contract and exchange may not lead to the employment of resources in their most valuable uses. In this situation, government might use its budgetary power to encourage the provision of those services that might otherwise be under-provided, thereby promoting the shift of resources from less valued to more valued uses. To say that government's budgetary power can be rationalized as being a means of promoting a more valuable pattern of resource usage does not, however, mean that government actually promotes such an end. The reality of taxation may be quite different than the rationalization given for it. The free-rider rationalization for government action envisages people paying taxes that would be equivalent to the prices they would have paid, if only contract and exchange could have been relied upon in the first place. Government action would, in other words, reflect a consensus that its pattern of resource usage was value enhancing rather than value diminishing, just as the choices of entrepreneurs in the market economy reflect such a consensus. To the extent that government provides effectively those things that cannot be provided privately because of the difficulties or impossibilities of relying upon property and contract, government participates in shifting resources from less valued to more valued uses. However, to the extent it does such things as preventing the development of exclusive and transferable ownership or expanding programs of public spending beyond levels for which consensual support can be found, government shifts resources from more valued to less valued uses.

It is one thing to develop a rationalization for governmental participation in the economy as being necessary to correct various market failures; it is a quite different thing to develop an explanation of the actual conduct of government. For government successfully to correct market failure, it must possess knowledge both of the existence of failure and of how to correct it, as well as possessing an incentive to act upon that knowledge. In recent years, scholars have begun to recognize that government may lack both the knowledge and the incentive to correct market failure. Indeed, government failure may well be more substantial than market failure, especially once it is recognized that much of what is called market failure really reflects a failure of government to permit the development of exclusive and transferable ownership. The reason why this is so is not because people in government have weaker characters, lesser abilities, or baser interests than people in private life, but because of differences in the types of institutions within which people operate. Institutions matter because they influence the pattern of costs and rewards to different types of actions. Market institutions tend predominantly to reward those actions that enhance the wealth of a society. Governmental institutions, in contrast, tend to reward to an important extent, at least under the system of majoritarian democracy, actions that transfer and erode the wealth of a society.

The Political Economy of Majoritarian Democracy

The system of majoritarian democracy that has evolved in the United States seems to clash with the basic requisites for economic calculation. This clash arises because governmental decisions concerning resource usage do not seem capable of reflecting a consensus as to the relative value of alternative uses, unlike the consensus that is implicit when resource utilization takes place within a regime of property and contract. Citizens cannot register directly their evaluations of public output through their choices about how much to buy. Instead, they must pay taxes regardless of the value they place upon what is offered. Likewise, political entrepreneurs are not residual claimants; they do not profit directly if they are correct in their judgment that a particular use of resources is value enhancing, nor do they lose if it is not. A system of tax finance in which a majority is able to make choices that compel the extraction of taxes from all is, as an examination of economic calculation under socialism reveals, a system in which a basis does not exist, either in knowledge or in incentive, for government to participate effectively in the process of shifting resources from less valued to more valued uses.

Despite a surface similarity, the ballot box and the market place are not equivalent means for ensuring that personal evaluations are reflected in outcomes, because property and contract do not operate in the majoritarian polity. If two candidates compete for office, voters will tend to support the candidate they think will more closely reflect their valuations. However, the support of only one-half the electorate is necessary under majority rule, and moreover, much recent work has explained why a system of majoritarian democracy often devolves into a system of rule by small but intense minorities. With majority rule, much of the cost can be placed upon non-supporters, so programs that shift resources from more valued to less valued uses might nonetheless be supported by the dominant coalition. For instance, had the Ford Motor Company been able to place much of the cost of Edsels upon taxpayers generally, as Chrysler was able to do 20 years later, it may well have continued the production of Edsels.

A simple illustration should suffice to make this point about the negative sum properties of majoritarian democracy. Suppose an entrepreneur thinks a nearby lake offers valuable opportunities for recreation and camping, so proceeds to assemble the necessary resources: the land, utility hookups, boats, water slides, and so on. All of those resources could have been used in different employments, but the entrepreneur has, by out-bidding other possible users, chosen to commit them to the provision of camping and water-oriented amusement. If the entrepreneur is correct in his judgment that his use of resources will be profitable, he will have succeeded in shifting resources from less valued to more valued uses, thereby making the other members of society better off at the same time he becomes wealthier. Should the entrepreneur's decision prove wrong and he makes a loss, the entrepreneur's employment of resources generates service of lesser value than some other employment could have yielded, and the other members of society will be worse off because of the entrepreneur's error. It is in no one's power to guarantee that a particular employment of resources will prove profitable, i.e., will shift resources from less valued to more valued uses. However the existence of residual claimancy or profit-and-loss does serve to concentrate the entrepreneur's attention on his decisions more strongly than would result if he does not bear this responsibility.

An entrepreneur's decision as to what kind of facility to create depends on his judgment about what people will be willing to pay for different types or sizes of facilities. The more he thinks they are willing to pay, the larger the investment that will seem warranted. Suppose it turns out that people will support a 200 acre facility, but not one of 400 acres, indicating that users will not be willing to contribute in admission fees enough to bid away the resources required for the second 200 acres from others who would choose to employ those resources differently. The creation of the 200-acre facility when none had existed before would represent a value enhancing shift of resources, but the creation of a 400-acre facility over a 200-acre facility would represent a value diminishing shift.

Suppose, however, that someone were to offer to pay 40 percent of the admission fee, meaning that a $5 ticket can now be bought for $3. Under this arrangement, the usage made of the facility would rise, possibly sufficiently so to justify a 400-acre facility. But where does the $2 discount come from? Within a system of majoritarian democracy, it can come from the nonusers of the facility. Assume for purposes of illustration that 60 percent of the population enjoys camping and water-type recreation, while the other 40 percent has little if any use for such activities. Further assume, to simplify the discussion, that the average income is the same for both categories of people, which in turn means that if government is financed by an income tax, the users will pay 60 percent and the non-users will pay 40 percent of the funds that are budgeted for the facility. In this case, users are receiving a 40 percent subsidy from the taxes paid by nonusers. The 60 percent majority is able to place 40 percent of the cost of the facility upon the minority. In such a situation, it is easy to understand why the winners on the issue of the provision of the campground and park will choose a larger facility than if they had to bear all of the costs themselves. As compared with a 200-acre facility, the 400-acre facility represents a shift of resources from more valued to less valued uses. But there is no entrepreneur who loses wealth as a result of making the decision to commit resources to the larger facility, because the loss of wealth is diffused over all of the taxpayers whose tax payments to finance the facility exceed the value they place on the facility.

But is it proper to compare the decisions taken by private entrepreneurs and public officials according to some standard of profitability? Some might wonder whether the single-minded promotion of economic calculation would not represent the elevation of economics to the focal point of ultimate value. Fortunately, however, there is no real conflict between "monetary" concerns and "humane" concerns. In a well-ordered society, people are, as Samuel Johnson noted, seldom so innocently engaged as when they are making money. And, as a corollary, it might be added that in a well-ordered society people are seldom so destructive as when they are losing money. After all, to say that a particular commitment of resources makes a loss means that those resources are used to satisfy wants that are valued less highly than those wants that could have been satisfied with an alternative employment of those resources. To make a profit, by contrast, means that resources have been moved from employments where they satisfy wants that are valued less highly to employments where they satisfy wants that are valued more highly. What is the significance of losing $1 billion? At a daily wage rate of $50 and a work year of 250 days, this loss represents the waste of 20 million days of people's time, which amounts to the waste of 80,000 people for one year. The loss of $1 billion is as if the annual work of 80,000 people were simply somehow destroyed.

Concerns of profit-and-loss are not properly set against concerns of humanity; there is no dualism of business and life. Economic calculation aids in avoiding the waste of people's efforts. As a result of more effective calculation, a society is better able to avoid the ineffective employment of people's talents and efforts. Profit-and-loss is simply an indicator of the success with which human concerns have been achieved, and it implies no evaluation of those concerns. A concern with expanding economic calculation and with assessing institutions in terms of their ability to facilitate calculation reflects a concern to expand the effectiveness of human conduct in attaining desired ends, recognizing all the while that the evaluation of those ends is a separate matter having nothing to do with the virtues of profit or the vices of loss.

The qualifier "well-ordered society" does, of course, set aside numerous difficulties. For instance, a chemical manufacturer that is able to dump wastes in an unowned river will calculate differently than it would if the river were owned, in which case it would have to buy the owner's permission to discharge its wastes. So long as there exist defects or holes in the legal order, a standard of profitability will not necessarily ensure that more highly valued uses of resources are being promoted over less highly valued uses. What may appear to be a more highly valued use of resources to a particular firm may not be so if the firm has to take other factors into consideration, but which it need not consider because of holes in the legal order. Recognition of this problem is not, however, an argument against the promotion of economic calculation in society, but on the contrary is further testimony to the importance of institutions that promote calculation, in this case in the form of plugging the holes in the legal order that would otherwise hinder proper calculation.

Majoritarian democracy leads to the use of government as a vehicle for transferring wealth. Expansion in government is the means by which the transfers take place between the winners and the losers. The winning majority will tend to receive a dominant share of the benefits of the spending programs it enacts, while having the minority bear most of the taxes; the particular illustration of the campground and park used above has general validity as an illustration of majoritarian democracy. A negative-sum expansion in government takes place because this expansion provides net benefits to the members of the winning, majority coalition. Furthermore, as the scope for acquiring wealth through transfers expands, there will be a shift of resources away from the production of wealth into the pursuit of transfers. Any shift of resources from pursuing the creation of wealth to securing—as well as guarding against—the transfer of wealth will further promote the erosion of wealth.

The negative-sum expansion of government results because of certain asymmetries in prevailing political institutions. There are asymmetries both between the locus of the costs and benefits of government programs and between the knowledge held by the gainers and the losers of public spending programs. The benefits are generally more concentrated than the costs, which will tend to give gainers a stronger interest in supporting government expansions than it gives losers an interest in opposing such expansion (or in supporting contraction). Relatedly, the transmission of knowledge about the benefits to beneficiaries from particular programs is easier than is the transmission of knowledge of the more diffused harm done by such programs. It is, for instance, generally easier to inform potential beneficiaries of a proposed campground and park of the benefits they will receive than it is to inform the others of the costs to them of the program, say in terms of the lower tax bill they could otherwise have. Alternatively, it is easier to inform domestic automobile producers and the United Auto Workers union of the benefits they will receive from the enactment of a program to limit Japanese imports than it is to inform citizens generally of the costs to them of the program, say in terms of the higher prices of cars and the higher taxes that will be imposed on them.

The survival of protectionist legislation has long served to illustrate how biases in the intensity of interest among people can lead to negative-sum programs. While the losses to consumers exceeds the gains to producers, the concentrated interest of producers dominates the diffused interest of consumers. Producers of beef would rationally organize to secure restrictions on imports because an increase in the price of beef would raise substantially their real income. Consumers, however, spend on many products, so a rise in the price of beef would bring about only a relatively small reduction in their real incomes. While it would be in the interest of all consumers acting together to oppose the protectionist legislation, there is no incentive for any one consumer to act independently to do so because most of the benefits would accrue to other consumers. In these and in other ways, an asymmetry within the political system enhances the survival value of negative sum programs that transfer wealth to the winners in the process.

Consensual Democracy and the Common Welfare

The various asymmetries that have been noted above, as well as others that have been discussed in various writings, are all reflections of one fundamental asymmetry: the absence of a *quid pro quo* relationship between the claims government places upon citizens and the services it renders to them. Those who have no use for the campground and park must pay for it anyway; those who would like to use it can do so without paying for it to the extent they can place the cost on others. Majoritarian politics necessarily reduces in significant measure to designing policies that take from some citizens to give to others, possibly with those in control of the offices of government claiming a brokerage commission in the process. This negative sum feature of majoritarian democracy was recognized nearly a century ago by Knut Wicksell.[3] Wicksell recognized, as did the authors of the *Federalist Papers* before him, that factional or majoritarian democracy is a vehicle for the creation of externalities. Recall the illustration of the factory that emits smoke and soot. That factory places part of the cost of its output on its neighbors, which means that the price of its product is lower than it would be if the damage done by the smoke and soot were incorporated into the price of its product. Within majoritarian democracy, the winners on an issue are analogous to the customers who get a lower price because part of the cost is placed on others, and the losers are analogous to the owners of property adjacent to the factory, and who, through their higher expenses for laundering and painting, are actually paying part of the price for those who purchase the factory's output.

There has been a growing awareness in recent years of the negative sum properties of contemporary democracy that arise from the absence of a *quid pro quo* relationship between the taxes that are taken from people and the services that people receive from government. In turn, remedy would seem ultimately to require the formation of an institutional order consistent with such a *quid pro quo* relationship, within a system of what can be called consensual democracy. The seminal contribution to consensual, as against majoritarian, democracy was, as mentioned above, made by Knut Wicksell, who attempted, in terms of the constitutional monarchy of Sweden in 1896, to describe an alternative institutional order that was both reasonable and which would create a *quid pro quo* relationship between citizens and government. By doing this, Wicksell was suggesting a way of putting into practice the dictum that government should be based on the consent of the governed. Within a legislature that was truly representative of the citizenry, consensus within the legislature would reasonably indicate consensus within the citizenry. As for the legislature, a pristine form of consensual democracy would be government by unanimity. Wicksell recognized, however, that unanimity would be exceedingly difficult to attain, and that a small movement away from unanimity would still essentially involve concord rather than discord or faction. To this end, he suggested that some voting rule within the legislature on the order of 75 to 90 percent would be

---

[3] Knut Wicksell, *Finanztheoretische Untersuchungen* (Jena: Gustav Fischer, 1896). The pertinent sections are translated as "A New Principle of Just Taxation," in *Classics in the Theory of Public Finance*, ed. by Richard A. Musgrave and Alan T. Peacock (London: Macmillan, 1958), pp. 72–118.

reasonable and effective. In conjunction with this voting rule, Wicksell described a set of procedures for reaching budgetary decisions, in which any proposal for government expenditure would require the sponsors also to propose a means of paying for the program, for otherwise it would be impossible for people to judge whether what they were getting was worth what they were being asked to pay.

The use of resources in value enhancing rather than in value diminishing uses is possible only within a consensually-oriented order, referring to the polity as well as the economy, for it is the consensual property of an institutional order that promotes value enhancing uses of resources. Without some type of consensual order that applies both to businesses and to governments, the negative sum activities of government seem inevitable. Consensual democracy essentially injects property and contract into the relationship between citizens and government, thereby making economic calculation possible. As a result, government becomes subject to the same rules of economical conduct as private citizens, rather than remaining outside those rules, as it does under majoritarian democracy. Wicksell recognized that there was an incongruity between prosperity and majoritarian democracy, and also recognized that this incongruity stemmed from the incentives inherent in majoritarian democracy. Seen in this light, the approach to a remedy became clear: the institutional order within which government operates must be changed so as to replace the incentives for engaging in tax-transfer politics with incentives for engaging in wealth creation politics. This can only be done within a consensual democracy, for it is only through consensus that economic calculation can take place. Hence, the next order of business becomes the practical implementation of consensual democracy, which Wicksell approached within the framework of the constitutional monarchy of his time.

Before giving further consideration to consensual democracy, it should perhaps first be noted that it is commonly argued that the economic activities of private citizens and of government *must* be organized according to different principles. While market activities are appropriately organized by contract and prices, the organization of shared consumption through government requires the compulsion of tax finance. If the organization of such activities is left to contract, some people will be free riders, it is commonly argued, and the absence of their contributions will lead to under-provision of the items of shared consumption, and this possibility of under-provision is used to rationalize the compulsory extraction of taxes as being necessary and proper for overcoming the free-rider problem.

This presumption about free riding may, however, be as misleading as it is common. For instance, experimental work by Peter Bohm finds that people generally reveal their preferences rather than trying to free ride in cases where there are efforts to organize the provision of shared consumption activities through contract instead of through compulsion.[4] As Earl Brubaker has argued in trying to explain this discrepancy between Bohm's experimental study and the intuitive hunches of most of the literature on public goods, what may be dominant in people's minds is not a desire to free ride as such, but rather a desire simply to be assured that they will not be fleeced by those who may free ride.[5] In the typical formulations of the free-rider problem, those who are truthful about their evaluation of objects of shared consumption are forced to pay on the basis of those evaluations, and thereby are taken advantage of by those who are deceitful, who are, by professing to place no value on the service in question, able to escape payment.

However, if the underlying motivation is not to free ride, but is only to ensure against getting fleeced, a motivation which Bohm's experimental evidence suggests is dominant in these situations, free riding may create little problem. So long as motions to provide items of shared consumption take the general form that no facility will be provided, i.e., no taxes actually levied, unless the sum of expressed individual desires to contribute exceeds some specified amount, people who are truthful in expressing their preferences will not be harmed significantly by those who are not. Through the use of some such form of "pre-contract excludability," to use Brubaker's term, the free-rider problem might be largely overcome within the public sector, and with consensus coming to guide the utilization of resources by government.

Indeed, the generally ignored problem of the forced rider, from whom taxes are extracted in excess of any value received, may be more severe than the problem of the free rider. Regardless, it so happens that both the free-rider problem and the forced-rider problem can both be largely overcome through some form of consensual democracy for organizing the provision of shared consumption. As Brubaker notes:

> The opportunities for eliciting more nearly voluntary economic expression of individual priorities for collective goods may be far greater than most of the contemporary orthodox literature suggests. If so, it may be eminently worthwhile to explore more carefully means to expand the scope of voluntary arrangements for provision of collective

---

[4] Peter Bohm, "Estimating Demand for Public Goods: An Experiment," *European Economic Review*, 3 (No. 2, 1972), pp. 111–30.

[5] Earl R. Brubaker, "Free Ride, Free Revelation, or Golden Rule?" *Journal of Law and Economics*, 18 (April 1975), pp. 147–61.

needs while perhaps in some measure of correspondence reducing reliance on coercive institutions with their own potentially detrimental effects.[6]

In a related line of analysis, Harold Demsetz has noted that there is no obstacle to the private provision of shared consumption goods so long as the entrepreneurs who organize the supply of such goods are able to exclude nonpurchasers from consumption. Moreover, the market process through which such goods are produced will result in essentially the same pattern of differential prices among people that accords with the dictates of the theory of public goods, and yet be consistent with the market process of contract and exchange, i.e., resource utilization through consensus.[7]

The organization of shared consumption through contract may encounter some difficulty, Demsetz acknowledges, when nonpurchasers cannot be excluded from consumption. Even here, however, there are opportunities for tie-in arrangements, in which the consumption of an item of shared consumption is tied to the consumption of something else. For instance, both advertisers and those who produce television sets have an incentive to see that programs are broadcast, and even in the absence of a technology to charge people for their usage of television signals, those signals will be provided. Admittedly, tie-ins for the provision of such collective goods may not be "efficient" when compared with some idealized, nonattainable setting of perfectly working government. But actual government, plagued as it is by forced-rider problems and operating within an institutional order (majoritarian democracy) that impedes effective participation in the process of moving resources from less valued to more valued uses, is much removed from perfection.

Indeed, such tie-ins were common before the development of modern techniques of tax extraction. Before World War I, for instance, it was not uncommon for revenues and profits from such government enterprises as post offices, railroads, and forests to form an important source of revenue for government budgets in European nations. Such enterprises made profits rather than losses, with the profits being used to finance other budgetary activities. Despite the vastly wider scope given to contract as a basis for organizing governmental economic activity in those earlier times, it would seem difficult to

---

[6] *Ibid.*, 158. For further thoughts about how this might be accomplished, see *idem*, "a Two-Stage Hybrid Mechanism for Collective Choice," *Public Choice*, 32 (Winter 1977), pp. 101–11.

[7] Harold Demsetz, "The Private Production of Public Goods," *Journal of Law and Economics*, 13 (October 1970), pp. 293–306. For further emendation of the issues raised by Demsetz, see Thomas E. Borcherding, "Competition, Exclusion, and the Optimal Supply of Public Goods," *Journal of Law and Economics*, 21 (April 1978), pp. 111–32.

claim that the scope for shared or common consumption was substantially narrower then. What mainly distinguishes those earlier times from our contemporary period seems to have been the substantial technological advances that have taken place in the ability of government to extract taxes from its citizenry. With those advances, the public sector expanded, and the state enterprises that formerly were a source of revenue now began to lose money and become objects of subsidization. This shift from profit to loss seems to have an understandable basis in the shifting incentives created by the developing technology of tax extraction. With the increased ability to extract taxes, government could run losses on its formerly-profitable enterprises, using those losses to confer benefits on favored groups who purchased the pertinent legislation, and with the losses being covered by taxation. With the development of taxation as the main means of financing the activities of government, ownership and contract as a basis for the organization of shared consumption by government came to be replaced by non-ownership and compulsion.

With respect to tie-ins between items of shared consumption and items of personal consumption, what, after all, is a system in which the profits earned from a railroad or a forest are used to build and maintain highways but a system of tying the purchase of a railroad ticket or a permit to harvest timber to the purchase of highway maintenance? Clearly this arrangement is not perfect as compared with some utopian idealization of public goods theory. In any comparison of realizable alternatives, however, the method of price and profit finance has the advantage of being more consistent with the essential requisites for economic calculation or positive sum conduct than is tax finance. If government is financed by prices and profits, majoritarian democracy will have been largely replaced by consensual democracy, for government's expansion will be determined by the relative valuations people place on the activities provided by government vis-a-vis those provided by private individuals. A system of government finance based on prices and profits is compatible with the basic institutional requisites for economical conduct — ownership and contract. Existing thinking about government has been oriented toward thinking in terms of two distinct principles of economic organization: contract, which would be appropriate for the provision of items of private consumption, and compulsion, which would be appropriate for the provision of items of shared consumption. But there is only one principle for effective economical conduct regarding the use of resources, and implementation of this principle requires some form of consensually-based institutional order.

A hotel, it is interesting and instructive to note in this regard, essentially represents the organization of shared consumption by consensus and contract. The corridors and elevators of a hotel are equivalent to the streets and sidewalks of a city; both are means by which people can get from place to place. Just as numerous questions can be raised concerning the allocation of resources to streets and sidewalks, so can the same list of questions be raised with respect to corridors and elevators. Both can be kept more or less clean, more or less brightly lit, and constructed of a lesser or a higher quality. Likewise, cities and hotels both provide for open spaces of varying types; again, a decision is made in both instances as to how many resources to devote to such objects of shared consumption. Moreover, hotels, like cities, typically contain a variety of stores and shops that provide services for private consumption. Indeed, a hotel offers a tied package of private consumption and shared consumption. Such communal services as police, fire, sanitation, recreation, and transportation are in effect provided by the profits earned from such private services as rooms, meals, and shops. In a hotel, the provision of communal wants takes place through contract, as Brubaker suggests is conceivable, is financed by tying their provision to the provision of private services, as Demsetz indicates is also possible, and, moreover, corresponds to the way governments largely were financed before the development of modern techniques of tax extraction.

A Constitutional Framework for Consensual Democracy:
A Forward Look

It is common and comforting to believe that the negative sum predicament of contemporary democracy can be escaped by electing the right politicians who will then enact a new deal, a fair deal, a great society, a new beginning, or whatever other characterization may be part of their effort to carve out a winning, majority coalition. A careful examination of majoritarian democracy suggests, however, that the erosion of wealth and liberty results not from bad people but from the incentives ordinary people confront within the prevailing system of majoritarian democracy. If so, what would seem needed to offset this erosion is not so much a change in the composition of the legislature as a change in the constitutional framework within which government governs. Within the system of majoritarian democracy, government cannot provide for the common welfare because there is neither the knowledge necessary to assess whether the common welfare is being promoted nor the incentive to promote it. Instead, government is more properly understood as an entity that is rewarding some, penalizing others, and squandering resources in any event.

Within the classical liberal view of the nightwatchman state, government is viewed as the umpire for the market economy, but not as a participant in the economy, save only to the extent that it participates only where people cannot provide effectively for themselves, begging all quesions of how such limited participation can be consistent with the incentives contained within such a constitutional order. Politics and economics are treated as belonging to distinct spheres of activity, in which each sphere possesses its own rules and institutions. Once economics and politics are recognized as constituting inseparable spheres of human conduct, the idea of separate rules and institutions for each sphere cannot be maintained. A unified treatment of political economy becomes necessary. So long as the economic order rewards only positive sum uses of resources while the political order rewards negative sum uses as well, the political order will be used to reward negative sum actions in the economic order. Again, there is the saga of domestic automobile companies engaging in negative sum transformations of resources which buyers reject in favor of foreign products, with the companies then buying legislation to restrict imports, which compounds the negative sum character of the episode. So long as government is organized according to majoritarian principles, its participation in the economy will involve negative sum, tax-transfer elements because there are profits to successful special interests and to politicians from the supply of such legislation.

Much work remains to be done on the organization of shared consumption through a constitutional order that can be characterized as consensual democracy. What is of enduring value in Wicksell's contribution to the theory of political economy, as well as that of the authors of the *Federalist Papers*, is not the suggested form of consensual democracy, but the recognition that government can act as a value-enhancing participant in the division of labor in society only to the extent the polity and the economy both operate within essentially the same, consensually-oriented institutional order. In the present age, there are probably numerous ways in which democractic institutions may become consensually oriented. Certainly, the power to tax would have to be severely curtailed in a consensual democracy, though the purpose of this curtailment would be not to limit the size of government *per se*, but to replace compulsion and dissensus with contract and consensus in the organization of shared consumption. At the same time, government would have to be based in some manner on the appropriability of the profits that result from its positive sum participation in the division of labor, and there would have to be some locus of responsibility for the losses that result from negative sum participation. In this regard, the recent development of interest in demand revelation and in related methods by which political outcomes may reflect the consensual valuations of citizens is of great interest. All of these methods suggest ways in which citizen evaluations of policies and programs can be brought more meaningfully to bear on outcomes, and advance means by which legislators will operate within a framework of residual claimancy.

The fundamental truth of supply side economics is that production takes precedence over consumption in economic life. Wants are unlimited, so there is no problem of stimulating the wants of people. It is the ability to produce that is limited, and the primary social problem is to facilitate rather than to hinder this ability. Government has several essential roles to play as a participant in the division of labor in society. However, the system of majoritarian democracy that has evolved also leads to a variety of negative sum, wealth-eroding activities of government. The growing interest in supply side economics reflects a growing recognition of various wealth-eroding activities of government. To an important extent, the reasons for those wealth-eroding activities reside in the incentive system of majoritarian democracy, and to create a framework in which government has a predominant incentive to act as a wealth-creating participant in the division of labor in society, as against acting as a wealth-transferring and, hence, wealth-eroding participant, requires that government also act within some consensually-oriented framework of property and contract, rather than in contradiction to it. Regardless of particular features of different institutional possibilities, what is of central importance is that the problem of social order be approached not from the perspective of separate spheres for politics and economics, but from the perspective of a unified political economy. As for what specifically might constitute a workable framework for consensual democracy in the present age, this is mainly a task for future research and for a far lengthier work than this short essay.

SUGGESTIONS FOR FURTHER READING

Economic calculation is explored in Friedrich A. Hayek, *Individualism and Economic Order* (Chicago: University of Chicago Press, 1948), esp. pp. 119–208. For a sympathetic exposition of the idea of a mixed economy, see James E. Meade, *The Intelligent Radical's Guide to Economic Policy* (London: Allen and Unwin, 1975). For a strong critique of that idea, see Steven C. Littlechild, *The Fallacy of the Mixed Economy* (London: Institute of Economic Affairs, 1978). For a critical examination of the failings of many of the common illustrations of externalities, with particular reference to bees, see Steven N.S. Cheung, "The Fable of the Bees: An Economic Investigation," *Journal of Law and Economics* 16 (April 1973), 35–52, and also the works of Coase and Knight cited in fn. 1 above.

The modern literature on public goods dates from Paul A.

Samuelson, "The Pure Theory of Public Expenditure," *Review of Economics and Statistics* 35 (November 1954), 387-89. For other contributions to that literature, see James M. Buchanan, *The Demand and Supply of Public Goods* (Chicago: Rand McNally, 1968), and the references cited therein. For an important contemporary contribution to consensus and democracy, one that builds upon Knut Wicksell's work, see James M. Buchanan and Gordon Tullock, *The Calculus of Consent* (Ann Arbor: University of Michigan Press, 1962). A valuable historical study of the development of tax-transfer politics and the system of majoritarian democracy in the United States is Terry L. Anderson and Peter J. Hill, *The Birth of a Transfer Society* (Stanford, CA: Hoover Institution Press, 1980). On the benefit principle of public economics as an approach to consensual democracy, see Richard A. Musgrave, *The Theory of Public Finance* (New York: McGraw-Hill, 1959), pp. 61-89.

On the growth of government, see, for instance, Allan H. Meltzer and Scott F. Richard, "Why Government Grows (and Grows) in a Democracy," *Public Interest* 52 (Summer 1978), 111-18; Sam Peltzman, "The Growth of Government," *Journal of Law and Economics* 23 (October 1980), 209-87; Karl Brunner, "Reflections on the Political Economy of Government: The Persistent Growth of Government," *Schweizerische Zeitschrift für Volkswirtschaft und Statistik* 114 (September 1978), 649-80; and James T. Bennett and Manuel H. Johnson, *The Political Economy of Federal Government Growth: 1959-1978* (College Station: Texas A&M University Press, 1980). On the survival of protectionist legislation and related measures, see the development in Anthony Downs, *An Economic Theory of Democracy* (New York: Harper & Row, 1957); and the extension in Mancur Olson, Jr., *The Logic of Collective Action* (Cambridge: Harvard University Press, 1965). Some political reasons for the subsidization of public enterprises are examined in Sam Peltzman, "Pricing in Public and Private Enterprises: Electric Utilities in the United States," *Journal of Law and Economics* 14 (April 1971), 109-47. On the continuity of government participation in economic life, see Jonathan R. T. Hughes, *The Governmental Habit: Economic Controls for Colonial Times to the Present* (New York: Basic Books, 1977). On the organization of community by contract, see the interesting treatment of Spencer H. MacCallum, *The Art of Community* (Menlo Park, CA: Institute for Humane Studies, 1970). Demand revelation as an approach to consensual democracy is explored in Edward H. Clarke, *Demand Revelation and the Provision of Public Goods* (Cambridge, Mass: Ballinger, 1980). An interesting experimental study with a similar orientation is Vernon L. Smith, "The Principle of Unanimity and Voluntary Consent in Social Choice," *Journal of Political Economy* 85 (December 1977), 1125-39.

TAXATION, SAVINGS, AND LABOR SUPPLY: THEORY AND EVIDENCE OF DISTORTIONS

BY

MAI NGUYEN WOO

Mai Nguyen Woo is a Research Associate at the Institute for Research on the Economics of Taxation.

THE SUPPLY SIDE ECONOMIC MODEL IDENTIFIES TAXATION AS one of the principal policy instruments to accomplish the dual task of reducing public spending and stimulating private capital formation. In the supply side model, an income tax cut can alleviate certain distortions of economic choices, producing a possible increase in savings in the private sector, and at the same time, it can limit the growth of the public sector beyond the optimal level. A business tax cut can also stimulate new investments in plant and equipment by raising investors' after-tax rates of return.

Among those who favor limiting government's involvement in the economy, some argue for a switch from the existing income tax base to a consumption tax base, which they believe would promote the build-up of a large capital stock to pass on to future generations. Moreover, they would rather place the choice of what types of capital to acquire in the hands of individual savers and investors than in the hands of the government.

This paper examines how taxes interfere with the efficient market by changing relative prices. Taxes imposed on capital income and on labor wages distort individual economic choices between present and future consumption in the first case, and between work and non-market activities in the second. The costs of tax-induced distortions are a misallocation of economic resources and, eventually, a reduction in everyone's welfare. The first section of the paper presents an analysis of the effects of the income tax on the productive behavior of individual workers who are also savers and investors.

The second section examines our present tax system and its effects on saving and work effort. Because this system incorporates some features of the income tax and other features of the consumption tax, investors engage in tax arbitrage, which produces distortions. Opportunities for tax arbitrage arise when taxes on selected sources of income are reduced in an attempt to alleviate the distortions explained in the first section.

In the third section, the effects of inflation on the structure of relative prices and on the tax system are briefly considered. Legislators who try to correct inflation-induced distortions by selectively reducing taxes, it is argued, must be cautious. The effects of such changes on economic choices are at best unpredictable.

The concluding section examines the comprehensive consumption tax and its favorable effects on saving. The link between individual saving and the rate of capital formation is also clarified.

I. Tax-Induced Distortions: Theory and Evidence

The following analysis assumes an economic world envisioned by Adam Smith, in which the levels of goods and services demanded and supplied respond readily to price signals. We will consider the basic decisions that a representative individual, John Doe, would make: first, in a no-tax world, then under a system of lump-sum levies; and finally under an income tax.

Optimal Individual Economic Choices in a No-Tax World

Given the going wage rate and the limited number of hours in a day, Doe chooses some fraction (H) of a day for non-market activities labeled "Leisure," and uses the rest of the time for income-producing activities, "Work." Doe also decides to spend a portion (J) of this income now and to save the rest for future capital income, and ultimately, consumption. Because he has no tax liability in this hypothetical world, Doe encounters no exogenous interference; he makes his choices because they reflect his preferences and priorities. As a result, Doe enjoys an optimal level of satisfaction.

The fractions H and J, which vary from individual to individual, represent Doe's optimal choices between work and leisure, and between present and future consumption. He bases his decisions on the two sets of relative prices: (a) The wage rate is also the price of an hour of leisure; the latter, being a desirable commodity, he will demand in a larger quantity the lower the price, and/or the higher the level of income. (b) The market interest rate is also the price of present consumption; the price of one dollar spent now is the interest earnings of, say, 10¢ if that dollar were saved for a year and then spent.

These relative prices guide all individuals in the economy toward their best choices between work and leisure, and between present and future consumption given their preferences and circumstances. The aggregate consequences in terms of the total labor supply and the total amount of savings available for new capital formation are optimal, in the sense that the collective maximum satisfaction is realized.

Rationale for Taxation

It is generally accepted, however, that a market economy needs the services of a government to function. The definition and enforcement of private property rights, for instance, is critical to the working of markets. To maintain a public sector, real resources are diverted from the private economy. The government may levy taxes, create fiat money, and borrow at home and abroad to pay for its expenditures. These instruments and their combinations all have different effects on individual economic choices.

This paper focuses on the inefficiencies caused by taxation. The term "taxation" is used here in exclusion of lump-sum taxes. Lump-sum levies, such as a poll tax or a head tax, are theoretically non-distortionary, because their amount is set independently of the taxpayers' economic activities. Thus, they do not influence taxpayers' economic choices one way or another.

In general, taxation generates some "deadweight loss" as long as non-market activities or leisure are not taxable. Individuals can move from the taxed to untaxed activities. This loss of welfare and productivity is essentially sheer waste, because the taxpayers give up more, in terms of their satisfaction, than the pecuniary amount received by the tax-collector. The term "excess burden" is used to designate the difference between the taxpayers' welfare loss and the amount of tax collected by the government.

One concern in tax policy, then, is to construct and adopt a tax system that minimizes this excess burden. The first step is to understand what impact this undesirable side effect of taxes has on individual choices, particularly on decisions about whether or how much to work and save.

The Work-Leisure Choice: A Theoretical Analysis

A tax levied on labor income, in effect, lowers the net wage rate received by workers, thus introducing a distortion in the individual choice between the taxed activities (Work) and the untaxed, non-market activities (Leisure). Let us return to the case of John Doe.

In a world without taxes, Doe, being paid $10 per work hour, may choose among the following options: $0 income (Y) and 24 hours of leisure (L); $10Y and 23L; . . .; $120Y and 12L; . . .; $240Y and 0L. Suppose that Doe decides to work 12 hours: He earns $120 per day, and takes 12 hours of leisure. Doe thus reveals that he values an additional hour of leisure exactly as much as an additional $10 hourly income. Doe chooses this income/leisure combination because it gives him the most satisfaction of the feasible options.

Now suppose that the government levies a $60 lump-sum head tax against Doe. There is no change in the price of leisure relative to income; Doe merely feels poorer because of this debt to the government. In order to pay this debt, he is forced to consume less leisure time as well as less income. This is the negative "income effect" of the debt. It reduces Doe's level of satisfaction (i.e. standard of living) by exactly the $60 handed over to the government. The optimal alternative chosen by Doe is now $90Y and $9L. He must work 15 hours, earn $150, pay $60 to the government, and keep $90. If the government in return provides $60 worth of public goods and services to Doe, there is no excess burden (or efficiency cost) here. In sum, the "income effect" of taxes causes individuals to adjust their income and leisure choice in the same direction: John Doe has less income and fewer hours of leisure than in a no-tax world.

In reality, most societies reject the lump-sum tax as inequitable, because it bears no relationship to the taxpayer's economic position. Instead, taxes are often based on "ability to pay": An individual earning more income pays more tax than one earning a smaller income. This principle of fairness is, here, assumed to be accomplished by a wage tax. Again, its impact on economic choices can be illustrated by the case of John Doe.

Suppose that $60 of revenue is needed and can be raised by a 50 percent tax on Doe's hourly wage. The net-of-tax wage rate becomes $5 an hour, and Doe's menu of income/leisure options changes to: $0Y and 24L; $5Y and 23L;...; $60Y and 12L; $65Y and 11L; $70Y and 10L; $75Y and 9L; $80Y and 7L;...; $120Y and 0L. Again, Doe reveals his preferences by choosing the $60 income and 12 hours of leisure option, which maximizes his satisfaction under these new circumstances. He works 12 hours and pays a $60 wage tax. Note that the $90Y and 9L option is no longer in Doe's range of choices, as it was in the world with a $60 lump-sum tax.

The tax on Doe's wage rate has reduced the price of leisure to $5 an hour. He gets more satisfaction for himself by substituting leisure for income up to the point where the last hour of leisure and the last hourly income are of equal worth to him, so he works 3 hours less than the optimal 15 hours in the lump-sum tax system. This is termed the "substitution effect."

This substitution effect represents the excess burden of the wage tax which has eliminated Doe's better choice and forced him to accept a lower level of well-being than under a system of lump-sum levies. Notice that Doe's labor supply remains at 12 hours under the income tax, the same as in the no-tax world. But as long as the substitution effect is non-zero, inefficiency exists, and is reflected here in the distortion of Doe's economic choices.

This loss of taxpayers' welfare beyond the loss of income was often ignored by policy-makers in the past, who put the emphasis on the net effect of the income tax on the aggregate labor supply. This tendency was reflected in a noted analyst's remark: "For many tax policies it would be sufficient to estimate directly the net result of the two opposing effects (the positive substitution effect and the negative income effect)."[1] In other words, a decrease in the net-of-tax wage rate normally induces a substitution effect unfavorable to work effort, and an income effect favorable to it. Conversely, an income tax cut increases the net wage rate, inducing a substitution effect favorable to work effort, and an income effect unfavorable to it.

Norman Ture argues that such an income tax cut results in no immediate income effect (see his essay in this book). The supply side analysis holds that whereas such an effect may occur for an individual, an aggregate income or wealth effect is impossible in the first order because the level of real government extraction remains the same. As a practical matter, in a world where information is not costless, some income effect may occur. [The rational expectations school has provided a basis for some income effect if information is sufficiently costly.] As Jerry Hausman wrote recently: "It is incorrect to measure the economic cost of a tax by its total effect on labor supply . . . (Suppose that) the 'size of pie' has increased because the tax has brought forth more labor supply. But still the individual's utility decreases because of the tax."[2] Our John Doe example shows this excess burden of the income tax via the non-zero substitution effect.

Most supply side economists accept the hypothesis that the effect of the current U.S. income tax system has been to decrease the labor supply. In other words, supply siders believe that the substitution effect outweighs the income effect such that a reduction in income tax rates will, simultaneously, increase the aggregate labor supply and alleviate the deadweight loss caused by these taxes.

Concerning the effect of taxes on the aggregate labor supply, Harvey Rosen[3] took great care in defining "labor supply" to include (a) lifetime hours of work and timing of retirement, (b) intensity of work effort, and (c) its quality, which hinges on the incentive for investment in human capital. Aside from this qualitative issue, as far as tax-policy is concerned, the empirical question is narrowed down to

---

[1] George F. Break, "The Incidence and Economic Effects of Taxation," in *The Economics of Public Finance*, Essays by Alan S. Blinder, et. al. (Washington, D.C.: The Brookings Institution, 1974), pp. 119–237.

[2] Jerry A. Hausman, "Income and Payroll Tax Policy and Labor Supply," Working Paper No. 610 (Cambridge, Ma.: National Bureau of Economic Research, Dec. 1980) p. 12. Words in parentheses are added for the purpose of clarification.

[3] Harvey S. Rosen, "What is Labor Supply and Do Taxes Affect It?" *American Economic Review*, 70 (May 1980), pp. 171–76.

how large the substitution effect of the income tax on labor hours is relative to its income effect.

The Work/Leisure Choice: A Selective Survey of Empirical Evidence

As late as the mid 1970's, it could be said that: "Thus far, cross-section econometric analyses of the labor supply have failed to produce consistent estimates of the relative importance either of the income and substitution effects of taxation, or of the participation and hours-worked behavioral decisions, or of the total labor supply reactions of different demographic and social groups."[4] Fortunately, enough progress has been made in econometric methods and data collection, so that some statistics regarding the work/leisure choice have become available to serve as inexact but useful guidelines to tax policymaking. As the following chronological account of some econometric studies shows, the work disincentives inherent to the income tax system are not trivial. This efficiency cost (among other factors) should therefore be taken into consideration in designing prudent policies.

An early effort to supply information for tax policy was made by Marvin Koster[5] in 1966. Koster's study was based on some 1960 census data on male heads of households in the 50 through 65 age bracket, individuals who were approaching retirement age and thus could afford to vary their hours of work, at least more so than younger workers. While expressing reservations about the adequacy of his regression equations and acknowledging the shortcomings of the data, Koster concluded that the income effect outweighed the substitution effect. This conclusion lent support to the notion that there is a backward bending labor supply curve for males in this older age group. According to Koster's statistical study, the welfare cost of changes in relative prices (due to the income tax rate changes) of labor and leisure appears to be very small, except when it affects the labor supply behavior of married women.

A few years later Michael Boskin[6] published a detailed analysis of the determinants of labor supply using a large body of data taken from the 1967 Survey of Economic Opportunity. His model was designed to estimate the income and substitution effects of a change in the

---

[4]George F. Break, "The Incidence and Economic Effects of Taxation," in *The Economics of Public Finance*, pp. 189-90.

[5]Marvin Koster, "Effects of an Income Tax on Labor Supply," in *Taxation of Income from Capital*, ed. by A. C. Harberger and M. J. Bailey, (Washington, D.C.: Brookings Institution, 1969), pp. 301-24.

[6]Michael J. Boskin, "The Economics of Labor Supply," in *Income Maintenance and Labor Supply: Econometric Studies*, ed. by Glen G. Cain and Harold W. Watts (New York: Academic Press, 1973), pp. 163-81.

wage rate for various population subgroups. Thus, the effects of factors such as race, sex, age, and family status on the labor force participation and on annual hours of work were taken into account. His findings indicated that: (a) There was no wage income effect on the labor force participation for all population subgroups. In other words, when total income (or wages) changes, there is no evidence that individuals would change their decision to join the labor force; (b) For husbands, who formed the largest subgroup with the highest total income, there was no evidence of positive substitution effects. This is to say that when the wage rate decreased (increased), implying a decline (rise) in the unit price of leisure, there was no evidence that the husbands would work fewer (more) hours. Thus, husbands as a group appeared to have no significant response in terms of labor participation of hours to work to a change in the wage rate, and; (c) There was statistically significant evidence of modest positive substitution effects for all females, except prime-age white wives and female teenagers. The largest work disincentives were found for black elderly wives, black female teenagers, and white elderly wives, who were trapped in some form of a negative income tax, such as welfare or some other social transfer program.

Most recently, Jerry A. Hausman provided some rough calculations of the deadweight loss, while emphasizing the latter as the correct criterion of taxation evaluation, rather than output effects. His findings indicated that "the economic cost of raising a dollar of government revenue by the income tax is about 25¢ on the average in terms of lost welfare. The marginal cost of raising an additional $1.00 of revenue by this means is approximately 40¢. Thus, the economic cost of the income tax is substantial."[7] The Hausman estimates were based on coefficients derived from a labor supply model which took account of the progressive tax system, using a sample of husbands in the 25–35 age group in 1975.

The Hausman study concluded that taxes had an important effect on both labor supply and deadweight loss. His example was an individual who was a representative husband in this sample and whose gross wage was $6.18 per hour; his non-labor income was $1,266. The Hausman model predicted that he would work 2,367 hours per year if there were no taxes, and 2,181 hours in the current tax system. Thus, taxes depressed his desired labor supply by 8.2 percent. This deadweight loss was then calculated to be $235, or 21.8 percent of his tax liability and 2.4 percent of his after-tax income.

Hausman also showed that the deadweight loss rose rapidly with the market wage. He concluded: "If less expensive means to raise fed-

---

[7] Jerry A. Hausman, "Income and Payroll Tax Policy and Labor Supply," p. 3.

eral tax revenue do not exist, the large amount of redistributive expenditure by the federal government is being done at relatively high economic cost."[8] The Hausman study is important in that it explicitly takes the income tax variable into account. It brought contrary evidence to the old belief that taxation has almost no effect on the labor supply of prime-age males.[9] However, for policy purposes, the Hausman numbers on the tax-induced loss of welfare and productivity should be used with care, even if the only limitation of his labor supply model is that it did not treat the young or old workers, or the nonmarried individuals.

In sum, as techniques and data quality improve over the years, new empirical evidence of tax-induced efficiency costs emerges. One factor that produces more dramatic statistical results is the dramatic increase in the nominal total income of individuals due to inflation in recent years. This bracket creep phenomenon results in higher real tax liabilities, and higher taxes produce more discernible effects.

Other Work Disincentive Evidence

The efficiency cost of the income tax was analyzed above in terms of the loss in the worker-taxpayer's welfare. But this cost is compounded by the fact that the income tax obstructs the labor specialization process. In this process, aided by the functioning market, workers' skills are bid away to their best uses; in a world without taxes, workers are best off selling their skills and time, earning the income, and then spending it on other goods and services. Each person in society would then perform closer to their potential and make use of their time in the most efficient way.

When a tax on market activities is introduced, this efficient allocation of time and skills is disrupted. The tax creates situations where a rational worker would be better off performing do-it-yourself, nonmarket activities. For instance, a highly skilled professional today must decide whether to work an extra hour and earn $100 ($50 after-tax), or spend an hour painting his garage, a chore that could cost him $85 if done by a professional painter. If cost-minimization is his objective, he will paint, and society will get no tax receipt and also suffer a $15 net loss in productivity because he chooses to paint the garage himself instead of doing his normal work. A specific case involves married women in the work force.

In a family, a wife's decision to enter the labor force depends in part on *her husband's* wage rate and tax bracket. Studies that take this

---

[8]*Ibid.*, p. 22.

[9]Joseph A. Pechman, *Federal Tax Policy*, 3rd ed. (Washington, D.C.: The Brookings Institution, 1977).

into account show that married women are sensitive to and respond to changes in these taxes.[10]

June O'Neil argues that "the current system of income pooling for married couples reduces the incentives to work for married women. It is not just fewer hours of work, but also as a result of taxing the family as a unit, investment in human capital may be deterred. Thus as long as non-market work and leisure are untaxable...(using the family as a tax unit) will exacerbate the distortionary effect on market work versus home activities."[11]

We will turn next to the other basic individual choice, the choice between consumption and saving.

The Consumption/Saving Choice: Theory

A tax levied on income that includes interests, dividends, and other returns to savings and investment lowers, in effect, the net reward for delaying present consumption. By lowering the price of present consumption, the tax biases individual decisions away from the optimal ratio reached in a no-tax world, and toward a lower rate of saving for future consumption.

Thus, the market interest rate is the price of present consumption. Assuming that the interest rate per annum is 10 percent, the price of one dollar spent now is the foregone interest of 10¢ that could be earned if that dollar were saved for one year and then spent. Assume again that a 50 percent tax is imposed on this income; the effective price of that one dollar of present consumption decreases to 5¢. Such a decline in the price of one of the two alternative courses of action results, of course, in the now familiar substitution and income effects.

Let us continue with John Doe, who now has $60 after-tax daily income. Before the tax on interest income, his choices between consumption and saving until next year range from $0C_p$ and 66_f;...; to $60C_p$ and $0C_f$, where C_p and C_f represent present and future consumption, respectively. Assume that Doe decides to spend $30 now and $33 next year. This ratio, 30 to 33, is optimal to Doe in terms of satisfaction, or welfare, in a no-tax world.

After the 50 percent tax on interest income, Doe's choices change to $0C_p$ and $63C_f$;...; $30C_p$ and $31.5C_f$; $31C_p$ and $30.45C_f$; $32C_p$ and $29.4C_f$;...; $60C_p$ and $0C_f$. Note that his previous optimal choice, $30C_p$ and $33C_f$, is no longer feasible; the tax has distorted the relative prices of present and future consumption, and,

---

[10]Harvey S. Rosen, "Tax Illusion and the Labor Supply of Married Women," *Review of Economics and Statistics*, 58, (May 1976), pp. 167-72.

[11]June O'Neil, "Family Issues in Taxation," paper presented at Conference on "Taxing and the Family" (Washington, D.C.: American Enterprise Institute for Public Policy Research, Oct. 13, 1981), p. 8.

moreover, left Doe a smaller net income. Under this income tax, Doe picks the $32C_p$ and $29.4C_f$ combination, which gives him the most satisfaction in this restricted menu.

If the same dollar of revenue were raised by a tax that, by having their relative prices intact, had a neutral effect on Doe's choice between present and future consumption, he would have had a different menu of options, from which he would have chosen the $28.5C_p$ and $31.35C_f$ combination. This approximately represents the income effect of this neutral tax, which nevertheless leaves Doe with a smaller income for both present and future consumption.

However, under the income tax the relative price distortion shows up in the substitution effect: As the price of present consumption declines, Doe increases the amount of income allocated to present consumption, from $28.50 under the neutral tax, to $32 under the equal yield income tax. This example illustrates the case where the substitution effect outweighs the income effect; the net effect is negative on saving for future consumption. It is thus theoretically possible that the tax on interest income creates a bias against saving.

In the aggregate, saving could increase if it were not subject to tax, and potential future consumption would be larger. However, to the extent that some individuals have planned a fixed expenditure in the future, they may save less as the after-tax return to saving increases. There is, once again, a strong theoretical argument against strong first-order income effects; still the question of whether personal saving would increase or decrease following a reduction of taxes on its return must be resolved by empirical studies.

Nevertheless, the deadweight loss of the interest income tax is clear: John Doe loses more in terms of satisfaction than the $3 received by the tax collector. As long as the substitution effect of the income tax on returns to saving is non-zero there exists the undesirable efficiency cost. In Doe's case, this form of tax costs him the preferred option ($28.5C_p$ and $31.35C_f$) obtainable under an equal yield neutral tax. He is forced to choose the next best option ($32C_p$ and $29.4C_f$) under the income tax.

The Consumption-Saving Choice: Evidence

For the purpose of statistical investigation, the issue is the sensitivity of saving to the changes in its net-of-tax return. An existing body of literature suggests that the U.S. tax structure drives a wedge between the marginal rate of return to private capital formation and the after-tax rate of return to private saving, making the level of saving suboptimal.[12] This is another way of saying that the tax on interest

---

[12]George M. Von Furstenberg (ed.), *Social Security Versus Private Saving* (Cambridge, MA: Ballinger, 1979).

income and other returns to saving imposes a welfare loss on society. The size of this tax-induced inefficiency depends on how responsive saving is to the after-tax rate of return.

During the 1960's, many economists felt that saving was interest-inelastic. In other words, saving did not respond to changes in the interest rate. In his seminal 1964 paper, "The Measurement of Waste," Arnold Harberger[13] challenged this belief. But it was not until 1969 that Colin Wright[14] presented some detailed statistics. His method consisted of estimating a consumption function that related aggregated consumption figures to variables such as income, wealth, and gross and net-of-tax corporate bond yields. The income, wealth, and consumption data were taken from classic sources[15] such as the works of Raymond W. Goldsmith, Albert Ando, Franco Modigliani, and Allan Meltzer. Postulating that the responsiveness of saving to the interest rate was functionally related to that of consumption, Wright estimated that the interest elasticity of saving ranged from 0.18 to 0.27. This implies that a substantial substitution effect, and hence tax-induced deadweight loss, did in fact exist.

As to the earlier evidence on the magnitude of the substitution effect, George Break[16] reported that, compared to a proportional income tax, an equal yield flat-rate consumption tax would raise saving by 2.1 percent of the tax receipt in the short-run and by 5.4 percent in the long-run. In 1957, Richard Musgrave[17] estimated a 13 percent reduction in saving if we switched from a general sales tax to a federal income tax with the same yield.

Against this historical backdrop, Michael Boskin[18] found a relatively large and significant elasticity of saving with respect to the real after-tax rate of return. The Boskin study attempted to explain con-

---

[13]Arnold Harberger, "The Measurement of Waste," *American Economic Review*, 54 (May 1964), pp. 58–76.

[14]Colin Wright, "Saving and the Rate of Interest," in *The Taxation of Income from Capital*, ed. by A. C. Harberger and M. J. Bailey (Brookings Institution, 1969), pp. 275–95.

[15]Raymond W. Goldsmith, *A Study of Saving in the United States* (Princeton, N.J.: Princeton University Press, Vols. 1 and 2, 1955; Vol. 3, 1956); Albert Ando and Franco Modigliani, "The 'Life Cycle' Hypothesis of Saving: Aggregate Implications and Tests," *American Economic Review*, 53 (March 1963), pp. 55–84; Albert Ando and E. Cary Brown, "Lags in Fiscal Policy," *Stabilization Policies*, Prepared for the Commission on Money and Credit (Englewood Cliffs, N.J.: Prentice-Hall, 1963), pp. 97–163; Allan H. Meltzer, "The Demand for Money: The Evidence from the Time Series," *Journal of Political Economy*, 71 (June 1963), pp. 219–46.

[16]George F. Break, "The Incidence and Economic Effects of Taxation," in *The Economics of Public Finance*, p. 194.

[17]Richard A. Musgrave, "Effects of Tax Policy on Private Capital Formation," *Fiscal and Debt Management Policies*, a series of research studies prepared for the Commission on Money and Credit (Englewood Cliffs, N.J.: Prentice-Hall, 1963), pp. 58–67.

[18]Michael J. Boskin, "Taxation, Saving, and the Rate of Interest," *Journal of Political Economy*, 86 (April 1978), pp. 53–527.

sumption in the 1929-69 period using variables such as the unemployment rate, household wealth, the inflation rate, disposable personal income, and the long-run expected real after-tax rate of return on saving. His results indicated that a higher rate of return would significantly increase saving; he put the elasticity of saving with respect to the real net rate of return at about 0.4. This is to say that a 10 percent increase in the real after-tax interest rate will bring forth a 4 percent increase in saving.

However, E. P. Howrey and S. H. Hymans[19] found no significant evidence of such a positive effect on saving in a similar time-series analysis. Thus, much of the contemporary discussion about the response of saving to the rate of return focuses on the technical merits of the two studies. Recently, a study by Lawrence Summers showed that "the common two period formulation of saving decisions yields quite misleading results. A more realistic model of life-cycle savings demonstrates that for a wide variety of plausible parameter values, savings are very interest-elastic."[20]

The Summers model postulates that individuals choose a consumption plan which maximizes their lifetime satisfaction while being subject to a lifetime finite budget. Thus, the aggregate saving rate is also determined by the age structure of the population, average life expectancy, the expected retirement age, and the rate of growth of output.

In this general equilibrium model, Summer estimated the efficiency costs of capital-income taxation, leading to these conclusions:

1) The income tax which distorts individual inter-temporal consumption choice has a large welfare cost.

2) The long-run responsiveness of saving to changes in the net interest rate is significant, and can be as large as a 19 percent increase in saving for a 10 percent increase in the after-tax interest return.

3) A shift away from capital income taxation to a tax on consumption can increase the Gross National Product by 10 percent, and

4) This shift would significantly increase capital formation and make possible long-run increases in real wages and, ultimately, consumption.

Notice that the appropriate measure of the efficiency gain of a tax exemption for saving is not the interest elasticity of saving, but rather the elasticity of future consumption with respect to the after-tax interest rate. What matters is the positive substitution effect of

---

[19]E. Philip Howrey and Saul H. Hymans, "The Measurement and Determination of Loanable-Funds Saving," in *What Should be Taxed: Income or Expenditure?* ed. by Joseph A. Pechman (Washington, D.C.: The Brookings Institution, 1980), pp. 1-48.

[20]Lawrence H. Summers, *Capital Taxation and Accumulation in a Life-Cycle Growth Model*, presented at the National Bureau of Economic Research Conference on the Taxation of Capital (November 16 and 17, 1980).

an increase in the after-tax interest rate on future consumption. In other words, if savings were exempt from taxation, individuals would save more early in life to pay for greater future consumption, and thereby improve their welfare even if total personal saving during their lifetime did not increase.

To repeat, the presently available empirical evidence on the deadweight loss of the tax on returns to saving makes clear that it exists, and that its magnitude may be substantial, even in a partial equilibrium framework. And when the potential of economic growth is taken into account, the deadweight loss of the capital income tax can be serious, as indicated in the Summers study.

Summary

In this section, the inherent distortions of basic individual economic choices caused by the income tax were discussed. The income tax encourages non-market activities over work-effort; it also encourages present consumption over saving for future consumption. The distortions show up in the non-zero substitution effect when the income tax lowers the price of leisure relative to work, and the price of present consumption relative to future consumption. The result is misallocation of resources, including capital and labor hours, and thus a loss of welfare to society.

II. Present Hybrid Tax System: Effect on Saving and Work Effort

The first section below explains how the pure income tax — based on the Haig-Simons definition of income as the sum of consumption and the change in net worth that accrues over the accounting period — causes distortions of individual choices between work and non-market activities, and between present and future consumption. This section will take a close look at the hybrid characteristics of the actual tax system, under which income tax and consumption tax treatments are applied to similar economic transactions. The present tax system fosters new distortions that appear in form like leveraged tax shelters, and which accumulate on top of the old deadweight loss.

The Present Tax on Individual Incomes from Labor and from Capital

In computing individual income taxes, income from all sources is pooled together and adjusted for income-producing expenses to calculate Adjusted Gross Income. Exemptions and deductions may then be subtracted to arrive at Taxable Income. From an appropriate tax schedule, an individual can determine his tax liability, from which he may subtract certain tax credits. The result is his net tax. Clearly, the types of adjustments, exemptions, deductions, and tax credits allowed in the U.S. tax code determine whether the returns to saving are taxed more or less heavily than the rewards of labor.

Some aggregate statistics may be helpful at this point. David Bradford[21] estimated that 19 percent of the national income in fiscal year 1977–78 may be classified as returns to capital, and 81 percent as returns to labor. Bradford also estimated average tax rates of 36 percent for savings, and 25 percent for labor and consumption. This also means that about 25 percent of the total federal tax receipts come from taxing returns to capital.

At first glance, these average tax rates seem to show that savings are taxed more heavily than labor income. But in fact there are other kinds of compensation besides wages and interest income, such as pension rights, in-kind benefits, and accruing changes in the value of assets ranging from common stocks to the inventories of proprietorships. These do not separate themselves into rewards to labor and rewards to saving. In fact, it is not possible to define wealth separately from labor. For instance, a man's labor results in a thriving business whose market value may depend upon his continuous participation in its daily affairs. He is laboring and saving simultaneously. It is also difficult, for tax purposes, to measure the changes in wealth on an accrual basis, these changes not being directly revealed by current market transactions.

Under present rules, some types of accruing wealth increases, such as capital gains, are not taxed, while some types of accruing wealth reductions, such as depreciation of business assets, can be deducted from adjusted gross income. Moreover, some types of returns to saving and labor receive the income tax treatment while other types of returns get the consumption tax system treatment. Hence, in general, the present tax system takes on a "hybrid" nature which tends to allocate economic resources in an inefficient way.

The Hybrid Tax Rules

The U.S. tax law tends to treat returns to saving more favorably than a Haig-Simons income tax. The Economic Recovery Tax Act of 1981 accentuates this tendency. Present laws accord special tax treatments to the following:

1) Long-term gains: Annual accrued gains in the value of certain capital assets such as common stocks, bonds, real estate, other real properties, etc... are not taxed. Only 40 percent of the total gains may be taxed when they are realized upon the sale of appreciated assets held over one year. Moreover, heirs of appreciated capital assets

---

[21]David F. Bradford, "The Economics of Tax Policy toward Savings," in *The Government and Capital Formation*, ed. by George M. Von Furstenberg (Cambridge, MA: Bellinger, 1980), pp. 11–68.

may set their cost-bases at the market value at the time of bequest. This, in effect, exempts from tax any capital gains accrued during the donor's lifetime.

2) The size of an estate passing on to heirs free from estate and gift taxes will be gradually raised to $600,000 by 1987. Also, the top tax rate on transfers in excess of $2,500,000 will be reduced to 50 percent by 1985. Moreover, unlimited amounts of property (with a few exceptions) can be transferred between spouses free of estate or gift taxes. Finally, real property used in a farm or other closely held business may be included in a decedent's gross estate at a value less than its fair market value. The qualifications for this special use valuation rule have been liberalized.

3) All returns in kind from household durables are untaxed. The most significant element in this category is the owner-occupied home; the related mortgage interest payments and real estate taxes are deductible from adjusted gross income. The homeowner is also allowed to defer the tax on realized gains upon the sale of his house if the purchase price of the replacement principal residence equals or exceeds the sale price. And if the taxpayer is over 55 years of age, up to $125,000 of realized gain on the sale of his home is not taxed. This is a once-in-a-lifetime privilege.

4) Limited contributions to qualified pension accounts, whether in the form of individual retirement accounts, annuities, bonds, or employer plans are deductible from adjusted gross income. All earnings of pension funds are exempt from tax, although pension payments upon retirement are taxed.

5) Investment in human capital is financed, in general, partly by foregone earnings and partly by net after-tax saving. The first part, foregone earnings, in effect, gets qualified pension treatment. This is because "increased future earnings financed through present earnings foregone are not taxed until they materialize. This implies that the interest on the deferral is not taxed. However, unlike earnings deferred to retirement years via a pension plan, the deferred receipts attributable to education are likely to encounter higher marginal tax rates than would have applied to the earnings foregone."[22] The second part, financing with after-tax saving, does not get the depreciation allowance accorded to physical capital, despite the fact that human capital, like physical capital, has a finite economic life. In this respect, investment in physical capital is tax-favored over investment in human capital.

6) Other favorable tax treatment of savings and investments:
    —The cash surrender value of life insurance policies is not

---

[22]*Ibid.*, p. 17.

taxed as income to policy holders; the proceeds to the beneficiary are not taxed when received.

— Interest on certain state and local bonds is tax-exempt. Between September 30, 1981 and January 1, 1983 individuals are eligible for a once-in-a-lifetime exclusion of up to $1,000 of interest earned on special "all savers" certificates.

— The first $100 of dividends ($200 for a joint return) is tax exempt.

The Mechanism of Tax Arbitrage

In order to learn about the way these hybrid tax rules work through a market economy, let us turn to the David Bradford model,[23] with two real investment sectors, A and B. Let us also start with a pure income tax system, where investment income is taxed at a flat rate tax of, say, 40 percent (with refunds for negative income), and interest payments are deductible. Under these pure income tax rules, the yield on real investment in both sectors will be the going market interest rate, say 10 percent. The after-tax return to saving for all taxpayers is 6 percent in equilibrium.

Now let us change the rules for calculating the income subject to tax in sector B, say, in order to encourage investment there. For instance, we will allow immediate write-offs of investment outlays. To compensate for the revenue loss, the tax is raised to 50 percent for all taxpayers. The original allocation of resources is no longer compatible with the new rules. While the interest rate and rate of return are equal in both sectors, the mixed income and consumption tax rules present an opportunity for tax arbitrage. Let us follow a Mr. Smart who is in the 50 percent tax bracket.

One of the many ways of realizing a pure tax arbitrage profit is for Mr. Smart to borrow $50 and add $50 of his rebate (because $100 new investment can be deducted from his adjusted gross income, thus "saving" the 50 percent tax bracket individual $50 in taxes) to finance a $100 investment in sector B at no out-of-pocket cost. From the annual gross return of $10, Smart pays $5 in interest charges and $2.50 in taxes on net interest income. The remaining $2.50 represents a pure surplus to Mr. Smart, who has sacrificed no consumption or other asset accumulation.

In response to the changed tax rules, resources are expected to flow from sector A into sector B, while the before-tax interest rate will change until no further tax arbitrage profit is possible. In the new equilibrium, the before-tax interest return to saving may be 12 percent, and the before-tax rates of return to investment are 12 percent in sector A and 6 percent in sector B. Another investor who bor-

---

[23] *Ibid.*, p. 42–43.

rows $50 at 12 percent and adds his tax saving of $50 to buy a $100 machine in sector B obtains a gross income of only $6. This is just sufficient to cover his interest payment on the loan, and leaves him with no surplus and no new tax liability.

The necessary condition in the new equilibrium is that the after-tax rate of return received by all investors is the same in all sectors. Otherwise, resources would still be flowing out of Sector A into the tax-preferred Sector B.

Note that in this simple example, investors and savers obtain the same net-of-tax return of 6 percent both before and after the change in tax rules. Harberger,[24] among other economists, has pointed out that a tax break to investors in one sector of the economy may not increase the rate of return received by them or others in the new equilibrium, taking into account the necessity of raising tax rates to obtain the required revenue. It is thus possible to construct models in which the net-of-tax return to savers is either increased or decreased by the same type of tax break.

Finally, the pure profit of tax arbitrage is a phenomenon of disequilibrium. If the objective is to shift resources from sector A to sector B, one of the policy alternatives is to give tax preference to investment in sector B. The possibility for tax arbitrage will accelerate the flow of resources into sector B. The tax arbitrage gain vanishes in equilibrium, so that the long-run policy concern is mainly the efficiency of resource allocation: How much subsidy (and thus resources) do policy-makers want to allocate to the tax-preferred sectors of the economy? The social benefits of such a subsidy must be balanced with the total efficiency costs of changing tax rules which alter the structure of relative prices in the market economy.

To repeat, in a flat-rate tax system, the predictable effect of introducing the consumption tax to real investment in some of the many sectors of the economy is inefficiency in the allocation of capital. In equilibrium, after the tax rules change, the above example shows that the before-tax rate of return to investment in sector A is 12 percent, and only 6 percent to the investor in the tax-preferred sector B. Thus, a gain in productivity can be expected if resources are shifted back to sector A. This will happen when investment in both sectors receives more or less the same tax treatment, whether taxation relies on the income-base or the consumption-base.

Some Efficiency Gain:

In section I, it was shown that the income tax results in a suboptimal level of saving for future consumption — an inefficiency. Policy-

---

[24]Arnold C. Harberger, "The Incidence of the Corporation Income Tax," *Journal of Political Economy*, Vol. LXX (June 1962), pp. 215–40.

makers may wish to correct this intertemporal misallocation of resources by granting tax-breaks to certain types of savings. The Economic Recovery Tax Act of 1981 contained many selective tax reductions for certain capital incomes (for instance, All Savers Certificates). To the extent that the selective tax cut brings down the overall tax rate on aggregate savings, there will be a flow of resources to savings and away from present consumption so there will be some increase in efficiency.

However, the magnitude of this gain may be small in the near-term because many types of capital, being tax-preferred (eligible for accelerated depreciation or safe-harbor leasing, etc...), do not immediately affect the individuals' internal calculus between present and future consumption. Relatively more effective, for instance, is the liberalized rule on savings which are put away in tax-exempt individual retirement accounts.

Finally, when individuals invest their savings, they respond to the selective tax incentives. It is possible that the tax incentives have some effect on the total volume of investment, but at the same time a large distortionary impact on its composition. In the words of Arnold Harberger, "Almost certainly, the effect of the incentives on the composition of investment was much stronger than their effect on its total magnitude."[25]

The Distribution of Tax-Shelters in a Progressive Rate Structure

In a hybrid tax system investors use leveraged tax shelters to finance an investment eligible for consumption tax treatment by borrowing under the income tax rules. An example: borrowing to purchase tax-exempt bonds. The deductible interest payment is shared by the government, but the return is not. If the cost of borrowing equals the bond yield, the taxpayer realizes a net tax arbitrage profit with no investment or new saving. The economic response in the marketplace is a reduced yield on tax-exempt bonds, for example. The political response is to limit the supply of tax-exempt securities and to issue rules restricting the deductibility of interest payments. All this adds to the complexity of the tax code.

Moreover, other problems develop as one goes from the flat-tax rate to a progressive tax rate structure. Beginning in 1982, the U.S. tax system will have marginal income tax rates from 0 to 50 percent.

---

[25]Arnold C. Harberger, "Taxation and Capital Formation in Business," *Tax Review*, Tax Foundation, Inc. (February 1971) p. 8. Also see Arnold C. Harberger, "Tax Stimuli and Investment Behavior" in *Tax incentives and Investment Spending*, ed. by Gary Fromm (Washington, D.C.: The Brookings Institution, 1970).

Except for this feature, the same simple model above is used in the following example. The initial equilibrium shows that taxpayers' yield on savings ranges from 5 to 10 percent. They are indifferent about portfolio composition among financial and real assets in both sectors A and B.

Now give the consumption tax treatment to real assets in sector B. For the moment, disregard the required increase in tax rates to make up for the lost revenue, since the focus is on the problem arising from progressive tax rates. It is clear that these new rules give no immediate tax arbitrage opportunity to taxpayers in the zero marginal tax bracket. For them the deduction of the outlay on a machine provides no tax saving. For the 50 percent tax bracket investors, the payoff from the leveraged tax shelter is $2.50, as in the above example, for each $100 worth of new capital equipment.

Note that the new equilibrium is reached when ownership of the tax-favored real assets, capital in sector B, is concentrated in the hands of the high bracket taxpayers. They are the only ones who can "afford" to take advantage of the tax arbitrage process. This process stops when they are indifferent to the choice between fully taxed interest and the effective yield on tax-favored real investment. Thus for these high-bracket taxpayers the real investment yield and actual after-tax return on savings are the same. For all other taxpayers, the rate of return on savings exceeds that on real investment. In 1981, the U.S. progressive tax system featuring a top 70 percent marginal individual income tax rate, was partially responsible for "real" rates of interest (net of inflation) that were very high by historical standards; it was responsible to the extent that the arbitrage activities described here had come close to a new equilibrium.

In sum, this simple model implies that all real capital will be owned by the highest-bracket taxpayers, leaving aside matters such as portfolio diversification, if only real investment is accorded the consumption tax treatment. This pressure existing in the present U.S. tax system will surely grow as the consumption tax treatment of real investment is extended in the forms of investment tax credit, lower capital gains tax, accelerated depreciation, etc.,...,while leaving intact the income tax treatment of borrowing and lending.

Some Realistic Examples of Tax Arbitrage

Pretend that you are a potential investor in the 50 percent tax bracket, who is shopping around for the best return to his savings (i.e. capital).

Let us start out by considering whether you should buy a one-year Treasury Bill or a one-year "all savers" certificate. Both are almost riskless, being backed by the government. As debt instruments, both are quite similar economically. Yet, the interest yield on the certificate, equal to 70 percent of the prevailing 52 weeks Treasury Bill rate, is tax exempt up to $1,000 on a single return ($2,000 on a joint return). The interest earned on the Treasury Bill is taxed in full at the federal level.

At this point, you know that you would do better to put some savings, say an amount X, that will bring back $1,000 in tax-exempt interest income, given the market rate of the "all savers" certificate.

The amount of tax saved can still be yours if you are willing to play the leveraged-tax-shelter game, and if you wish to use the X dollars saved for other purposes. In other words, you can discreetly borrow X dollars to buy the tax-exempt certificate, knowing that the interest paid on the loan is deductible.

This feature of our present tax system rewards the taxpayers at the upper end of the income scale for engaging, in general, in investment deals which give rise to both tax-free interest income and tax-deductible interest cost. It certainly distorts their portfolio choices, and thus leads to misallocation of capital.

Now consider whether you should buy stocks of a qualified domestic public utility corporation or stocks of other companies with equal credit-ratings. Again, being in the upper tax bracket, you should be aware of the tax consequences of your investment. Starting in 1982, an individual investor in the public utility stocks can exclude up to $750 per year ($1,500 on a joint return) if he plans to receive dividends in the form of common stock rather than, say, cash. This exclusion rule does not apply to dividends distributed after 1985. Contrast this to the $100 dividend exclusion per individual taxpayer who invests in other common stocks.

Again, if all else is equal, you know which stocks to invest in, those of qualified public utility corporations. Now you get the idea; a smart investor must acquire some knowledge of the present tax rules, then use his imagination.

To the extent that limits are put on the amount of tax-exempt interest and dividends, the intended capital flow into the tax-preferred industries is also restrained. However, the adjustments toward a new equilibrium still distort investors' choices and the relative rates-of-return to capital employed in different industries.

Finally, in a broader context, let us compare the present tax treatment of real property to that of financial assets, taking account of existing institutions.

a) Leverage: The tax rules permit full deduction of the interest costs for financing purchases of real and financial assets. For instance, mortgage interest payments and interest charges to margin accounts at brokerage firms are deductible from the investors' adjusted gross income. The difference is in the financial institutional set-up. The savings and loan industry provides long-term fixed rate mortgages to real estate ventures, while the commercial banks and brokerage firms vary their margin account charges according to the going market interest rates. Also, mortgages attach the real property itself as loan collateral, while stockbrokers make margin accounts available only to relatively wealthy investors who can handle sudden margin calls as stock prices drop.

b) Yield: The before-tax return to real property is the rental income net of expenses, and to common stocks the return is the dividend. After 1981, the first $100 of dividends may be excluded from adjusted gross income on single returns. Otherwise, rents on real property and dividends of common stocks are taxed at the individual marginal income tax rates.

c) Net-of-tax yield: During the adjustment period, the real property investment generates tax arbitrage. The capital gains tax treatment of real estate and common stock is also factored into their net yields. As the tax arbitrage process speeds up the flow of capital into real estate, the gross yield of rental properties available starts declining as prices rise relative to their rental values. Negative cash flows are accepted by recent real estate investors as long as they expect the continuing price appreciation (inflation will be discussed in the next section). This is, in effect, a device to transform a portion of current income into future long-term capital gains, and it is available in the current hybrid system. Its rise results in investments — such as real estate speculation, commodities straddles, etc., — with zero or negative social rates of return.

So, where would you have invested your savings, had you been in the top tax bracket?

In light of these tax advantages and existing institutional practices favoring investment in real properties, and to the extent that savers and investors in the economy have finite resources, the present U.S. tax rules divert excessive amounts of resources into the housing sector, at the expense of financial assets (such as bonds and stocks which represent equity claims on the stock of productive capital). As predicted by the model, the median value of an owner-occupied home in the United States rose by 177 percent during the 1970's while rents only rose by 122 percent, according to the 1980 Census.[26] Also, the gross dividend yield of common stocks tended to rise (when the dividend payout rate is relatively constant), by putting downward pressure on stock prices during the 1970's. The adjustment via

---

[26]Randolph E. Schmid, "Home Values Up 177% in Decade," *The Washington Post*, November 21, 1981, p. E4, col. 2.

tax-arbitraging proceeds until the net-of-tax yields on all types of investment are equalized for the investors in the highest tax brackets.

Summary

The present tax system, featuring individual income tax rules treating some forms of saving according to a consumption tax principle and other forms (especially borrowing) according to a Haig-Simons income tax principle, opens opportunities for profitable rearrangements of individual wealth portfolios. Inefficiency in the allocation of wealth results from bidding for the tax advantages; the social rate of return is lower in equilibrium in the tax-favored activities than in those taxed by adequate income measurement rules.

The net effects on saving incentives of the present tax system are unclear. As far as most individuals are concerned, taxes are still levied on the bulk of their interest and dividend incomes. For taxpayers who spend resources in seeking out the best tax advice and the most ingenious tax-shelters, the overall after-tax yield on their investments may rise, inducing them to reallocate their income away from present consumption. Thus, some intertemporal efficiency gain may result from the selective tax incentives.

The expected outcome of the hybrid tax system is inefficiency in the allocation of investment resources, distortion in individual portfolios, transaction costs incurred in achieving tax advantage, and the appearance, at least, of horizontal inequity. Because the tax-advantage is most valuable to those in the highest tax bracket, assets accorded consumption tax treatment tend to migrate to the portfolios of the high-bracket taxpayers. These "tax-arbitrage" distortions are intertwined with the inherent tax-induced distortions discussed in the previous section.

So far, the problem of inflation has been put aside. The tax rules were recently changed with an eye to correcting the bias against saving by according the consumption tax treatment to certain forms of saving. The effect against the bias has not been immediate, and may not be negligible. Yet, new inefficiencies and distortions have been set in motion. Let us now turn to the analysis of distortions arising from the attempt by legislators to use the tax code to compensate for inflationary damages that have burdened some individuals more than others.

III. Inflation and the Present Tax System

Usually, when the general price level rises steadily we have inflation, which inflicts a long list of real effects and costs on the economy.

As two noted economists, Stanley Fischer and Franco Modigliani[27] have pointed out, the magnitude of the damage done by inflation depends on the institutional structure of the economy and on the extent to which inflation is or is not fully anticipated. The chief welfare costs of inflation include resource misallocations caused by variability of relative prices and uncertainty about future price levels.

The tax system in the United States was designed for non-inflationary times. Such tax provisions as exemptions, standard deductions, and tax brackets are denominated in current dollars. The tax system is thus one of the "nominal" government institutions where real effects of inflation are felt. Other "nominal" institutions are parts of the private sector: nominal accounting methods, nominal annuity contracts, old-fashioned fixed-rate mortgages, etc.

High rates of inflation in the past several years have seriously distorted the tax system by changing the value of the individual income tax provisions, as well as the methods of measuring taxable net income. There are two main sources of inflation-caused distortions: a) The individual income tax rate structure is progressive: when nominal income rises, even when real income does not, real tax liability increases because taxpayers are pushed into higher marginal tax brackets (known as "bracket-creep"), b) The accounting and legal procedures used in taxing business enterprises are "historical": The ground rule of taxation has been to measure taxable net income in terms of historical dollars. Hence, the historical cost is the basis for depreciation deductions, and for capital gains or losses. The nominal interest paid is the allowed deduction. As long as the repayment of a debt is equal in historical quantity to the borrowed dollars, there is no income gain to the borrower even when accelerating inflation has decimated the lender's capital; no loss or gain is recognized for tax purposes.

Tax policy-makers tend to overlook the different types of distortion, whether they are inherent in the income tax (such as the bias against saving for future consumption), result from tax-arbitrage (such as real estate speculation), or are inflation-induced ("bracket-creep"). And they conveniently change certain tax rules to correct certain economic ills, without fully considering the side effects of these tax changes.

William Fellner and his associates deplored the 1975 Tax Reduction Act for combining the correction for inflation-caused overtaxation with a change in the basic tax structure "in a very confusing way...In order to avoid sinister moves in the dark on future occa-

---

[27]Stanley Fischer and Franco Modigliani, "Towards an Understanding of the Real Effects and Costs of Inflation," *Weltwirtschaftliches Archiv*, 114 (1968), pp. 810–33.

sions—that is, in order to separate corrections for inflationary distortions from intentional modifications of the basic structure—new procedures involving operations in the nature of 'indexing' would be required."[28]

In other words, if inflation is the culprit behind certain tax problems, it is better policy to devise appropriate means to cope with it, such as indexation, than to enact a selective list of distortionary tax-favors and reductions. In a recent paper, Stanley Fischer[29] carefully explained the issue of indexing and inflation. The general reluctance to adopt indexation (of prices, wages, bonds, and taxes) stems from the fear that indexing is itself inflationary. Fischer's examination of a cross-section of 40 countries suggests that indexation did not in general increase the inflationary impact of the oil price shock of 1974.

The difficulty with making piecemeal adjustments for inflation is illustrated by the case of the tax on long-term capital gains. In 1978, Congress reduced the tax by exempting a larger portion of realized gains from taxation. However, inflation is a complex problem precisely because the rate of price increase differs across the various kinds of capital assets. For instance, the average price of real estate rose faster than that of common stocks during the 1975-80 period. The simplistic policy of reducing the effective capital gains tax rates did not and could not address this inflation-induced problem. Moreover, it produced an unintended consequence: The lower capital gains tax rate interacting with a high rate of real estate price appreciation added more fuel to the already active speculation in the real estate market of the late 1970's.

Another problem of inflation is that it benefits debtors (at the expense of their lenders), who gain when the real value of their repayment in the future is less than that of their original loan. A mere tax cut does not address this problem, either.

Again, inflation was one of the reasons that Congress adopted the Economic Recovery Tax Act of 1981, which incorporated "indexing" into the tax code, though the provision will not be activated until 1985. In the meantime, this Tax Act will continue the policy of reducing the individual income tax rates to counter "bracket-creep." The Tax Act of 1981 also grants certain tax incentives to businesses, such as a liberalized Last In First Out (LIFO) method of inventory accounting and an Accelerated Capital Recovery System (ACRS). ACRS replaces the previous system of allowing only a slow deprecia-

---

[28]William Fellner, Kenneth W. Clarkson, and John H. Moore, *Correcting Taxes for Inflation* (Washington, D.C.: American Enterprise Institute for Public Policy Research, June 1975), p. 1.

[29]Stanley Fischer, "Indexing and Inflation," Working Paper No. 670. (Cambridge, MA: National Bureau of Economic Research, May 1981).

tion of assets with a new approach that severs the ties of depreciation to the useful economic life of assets. Businesses in general consider these new tax incentives to be necessary as partial solutions to the problem of inflation. Of course, most of the justification for ACRS was not concerned with inflation.

But Congress in 1981 still did not take account of the fact that some business-debtors also benefit from inflation when they purchase real assets with borrowed funds. A new owner of an existing apartment complex with a large mortgage, for instance, can deduct a more generous amount of depreciation under the new tax law.

The U.S. tax laws and high inflation interact to discourage certain types of investment; business investment in new plant and equipment is a good example. This interaction is complex and operates through different channels. Using the tax system to correct for inflation without full indexation creates easy opportunities for unproductive leveraged tax-sheltering activities. As Martin Feldstein has observed: "Because of the non-indexed fiscal structure, even a fully anticipated rate of inflation causes a misallocation of resources in general, and a distortion of resources away from investment in plant and equipment in particular."[30]

In sum, the latest changes in the tax code, aside from the vague provision on "indexing" in 1985, did not directly face the tax-related problems caused by inflation. The central, often-asked question is: "If we are to take account of inflation on the measurement of taxable income, should the reflection of inflation be across the entire board covering all the assets and liabilities and other factors affected by inflation, or should it be only piecemeal?"[31] While we recognize the inequity of the piecemeal approach, this essay focuses mainly on its economic costs, i.e., its inefficiencies. As the tax code stands, if inflation remains at high levels, it still pays for wealthy investors to channel their capital into the real estate business and away from other productive forms of business investment. Since a piecemeal approach involves selective tax reductions without a thorough treatment of the symptoms of inflation, it does not close the tax system against tax-arbitraging activities which, as we have seen, result in a misallocation of resources.

Let us now investigate how the ad hoc changes in the U.S. tax laws to correct for inflation can create a mismeasurement of income from capital, with ill effects for non-residential capital formation.

---

[30]Martin Feldstein, "Inflation, Tax Rules, and the Stock Market," Working Paper No. 403 (Cambridge, MA: National Bureau of Economic Research, Nov. 1979), p. 37.
[31]Stanley S. Surrey, "Our Troubled Tax Policy—False Routes and Proper Paths to Change," Presidential Address, *Proceedings of the 73rd Annual Conference* of the National Tax Association Tax Institute of America. (Nov. 17, 1980), pp. 6–7.

For businesses, tax accounting methods apply to four areas: 1) depreciation, 2) inventories, 3) financial assets and liabilities, and 4) capital gains.

In a period of inflation, conventional accounting tends to overstate real business profits because it does not account for a) the higher cost of replacing plants and equipment, and b) the rising cost of carrying inventories. It is often claimed that inflation thus overstates profits, which results in taxing businesses more than was intended. But, since conventional accounting also ignores the gain to indebted businesses when the real value of their financial liabilities is reduced by inflation, the net result of inflation on business taxes is unclear and unpredictable.

Roger E. Brinner and Stephen H. Brooks[32] compared the tax liabilities, defined as a percentage of the reported "book profits," to those tax liabilities, calculated as a percentage of the "adjusted earnings," for corporations during the 1956-78 period. The book profits were calculated by conventional accounting methods. The adjusted earnings differ from the book profits by taking account of the slow depreciation, the inventory valuation problem, as well as the reduction of real debts. It turns out that there was clear evidence of the volatile effects of inflation on the tax liabilities of business during 1956-78. The study found that investors had failed to recognize that the pure nominal appreciation of real corporate net assets were brought about by inflation. "By 1978, this...had depressed the stock market by at least 20 percent."[33] The authors concluded that "inflation has reduced the efficiency of equity markets by damaging the quality of traditional earnings information so that the market currently substantially undervalues corporate assets."[34]

Martin Feldstein[35] also showed that expected inflation and its interaction with the U.S. tax rules would depress the prices of equity shares and reduce the size of equilibrium capital stock in the affected industries. His conclusion is based on calculations that include the tax and financial variables and also recognize the important roles of debt finance and retained earnings. This partly explains the poor performance of the stock market during the 1970's.

In this case, a better cure for inflationary distortions may be general indexation. Preempting the leveraged tax sheltering games will require the indexing of both the basis for depreciation and the lia-

---

[32]Roger E. Brinner and Stephen H. Brook, "Stock Prices," in *How Taxes Affect Economic Behavior*, ed. by Henry J. Aaron and Joseph A. Pechman (Washington, D.C.: The Brookings Institution, 1981), pp. 199-240.

[33]*Ibid.*, p. 202.

[34]*Ibid.*, p. 201.

[35]Martin Feldstein, "Inflation, Tax Rules, and the Stock Market," p. 56.

bilities of indebted businesses that have depreciable assets. Since the LIFO method allows taxpayers to deduct the most current costs of goods against sales income, the method can be used for tax accounting only if the taxpayer used LIFO accounting in the measurement of net profits for financial statements. This is to partially offset the investors' persistent undervaluation of common stocks.

To summarize: The complex interaction between the present hybrid tax system (which accords the income tax treatment to saving and borrowing, for example, and the consumption tax treatment for certain investment incomes) and inflation calls for "extreme care" in making tax-law changes. General indexation is an imperfect solution to inflation-induced distortions. The best solution lies in a general reform of the tax system. A comprehensive progressive tax, whether income or consumption-based, is preferable to the present hybrid tax. The next section presents our arguments for a comprehensive progressive consumption tax in light of the political and economic realities of the 1980's.

IV. Conclusion:
Towards a Progressive Consumption Tax System

Having examined a least three tax-related sources of inefficiencies in resource allocation, this paper concludes with a proposal aimed at improving the present tax system. Recall that the first kind of distortion of the relative prices of work and leisure, and of present and future consumption, is inherent in the income tax system. The second type of distortion results from the tax-arbitrage opportunities under the current U.S. tax laws, which treat similar economic activities differently (some on the income tax principle, others on the consumption tax principle). The third type of distortion reflects the damages of inflation, which tax-legislators have taken it upon themselves to correct by means of haphazard changes in the tax rules. It must be recognized that all these distortions are entangled; they often interact and feed upon each other. So, where do policy-makers go from here? Before presenting our argument for a systematic move toward a progressive expenditure tax as a major component of the future tax system, some caveats are in order.

First, to the extent that consumption requires an income and therefore work effort, and because of the fact that non-market activities such as leisure are not taxed, a switch from an income tax to a consumption tax will not remove the distortion in individual choice between work and leisure.

Secondly, our focus here is on the issue of real capital formation in view of the general concern about productivity in the United States. In addition to the efficiency costs of the tax system being evaluated, however, there are other important considerations in any tax reform, such as the political climate, the revenue requirement, the issue of horizontal and vertical equity in taxation, and the problems of tax administration.

Opinions abound on the best way to increase the rate of capital formation. Some economists favor a targeted approach, directing incentives at physical non-residential capital. They make two arguments. First, proponents of this approach cite the existing biases in favor of residential housing at the expense of productive capital. This long-standing bias has resulted in a less than optimal composition of our capital stock. Secondly, these economists argue that the existence of international capital flows reduces the value of policies designed to stimulate personal saving. Arnold Harberger, for instance, has commented: "Unfortunately, the existence of the world capital market makes it difficult for the United States to increase domestic capital formation by increasing saving...So, if additional investment is the goal, the way to achieve it in an interdependent world economy is by stimulating investment rather than saving."[36]

But the driving force behind supply side economics is the idea that the tax code ought not to influence economic decision making. The desirable tax system keeps the distortions of economic decisions to a minimum, and thereby improves the prospect for economic efficiency and growth. Hence, as a general proposition, targeting ought to be rejected, except in cases of market failure. The most important criterion is tax neutrality. A neutral tax system would result in economic decisions that are made without reference to that system. No perfectly neutral system is possible, but policy makers should strive for a tax system that least disturbs the highly competitive and efficient economy. This leads directly to our policy recommendation.

More often than not, different policy recommendations stem from different philosophical views of how the U.S. economy works. From our perspective, replacing the existing tax rules with a broad-based progressive consumption tax is very desirable because of the efficiency gains it would bring.

In view of the less distortionary nature of the consumption-based tax relative to the existing "hybrid" income tax, consumption deserves serious consideration as an alternative ideal for the tax base. The other ideal is the pure income tax base, which is unlikely to be adopted because it is extremely difficult, politically, to take away

---

[36] Arnold Harberger, "Comment" in *What Should be Taxed: Income or Expenditure?* ed. by Joseph A. Pechman (Washington, D.C.: The Brookings Institution, 1980), pp. 118–119.

tax-privileges from special interest groups. Proponents of the consumption tax argue that a reduction in taxes on personal saving would help build up a larger private capital stock (whether residential or industrial, etc.) for the benefit of future generations. Even if some capital is invested abroad now, the returns to it will still benefit the home economy. Besides, in view of the public perception that government is too big, the political climate today would seem to favor individual choice of the forms of additional capital stock over government choice. One way of returning this economic choice to the private sector is to stimulate personal saving by cutting taxes.

Hence, the consumption-based or progressive tax on individual spending is a timely and useful substitute for the present tax on individual income. A consumption tax differs from an income tax in that it excludes savings from the tax base. This means that, for a taxable year, net saving and gifts made are subtracted from gross receipts to compute the tax base. On the other hand, withdrawals from savings, gifts, and bequests received but not added to savings, are included in gross receipts to compute the tax base.

The 1977 U.S. Treasury Blueprints for Basic Tax Reform show that a version of a consumption-based tax, called the "cash flow tax," has several efficiency advantages over a comprehensive income tax. However, on the matter of equity in taxation, proponents of the consumption tax and those of the income tax disagree on the basic question of whether expectations (based on the life-cycle view) or outcomes (an ex-post view) are the correct building block. The income tax links the notion of equity and progression to the ex-post economic position of the taxpayer in any one year. The cash flow tax treats alike all individuals who begin their working years with equal wealth and the same present value of future labor earnings. However, an additional tax on wealth, for instance at death, can supplement the cash flow for an ex-post approach to tax equity.

The efficiency gains of a consumption-based over an income-based tax are: First, by removing the interest income tax on investments for as long as they are saved, the cash flow tax eliminates disincentives to saving, i.e., the distortion of relative prices of present and future consumption. Even if personal saving is totally unresponsive to the increase in the after-tax rate of return, the switch to the consumption-based tax would increase welfare by more efficiently allocating consumption over a lifetime. To the extent that the consumption tax increased the saving rate, it would encourage capital formation, leading to higher rates of economic growth, more capital per worker, and higher before-tax wages.

Second, the cash flow tax avoids the most difficult problem of income measurement under the present tax laws. These measurement problems are partly what have motivated various special interest groups to exert political pressure on Congress to change the tax rules to the detriment of the comprehensive income tax base. Some of these problematic elements are depreciation rules, inflation adjustments, and the allocation of undistributed corporate income. Under the cash flow tax, all forms of saving, including the above, would be excluded from the tax base.

And, as the realists would have it, it is recognized that any progressive consumption-based tax likely to be adopted in the near future would not be exactly the ideal model "cash-flow" tax. But it has a good chance of being less imperfect than the "hybrid" income system that presently fosters high interest rates, distorts economic choices, and condones unproductive, leveraged tax shelters.

Finally, regarding the three types of economic distortions related to our present tax system, this paper concludes that:

a) The income tax bias against saving for future consumption can be eliminated by adopting a consumption-based tax.

b) The resource misallocation caused by the present hybrid tax system via the tax-arbitrage mechanism can be corrected by adopting a broad-based tax, whether income or consumption. It is more realistic, however, to go forward to the progressive consumption tax, considering the present political climate.

c) The distortions and inefficiencies caused by inflation and its interaction with the existing tax system must be dealt with at its source — by curing inflation, or at least by general indexation (including tax-indexation) if no other better symptom treatment is available. Most inflation-related distortions would be eliminated under a comprehensive, progressive consumption tax system.

FROM ANTITRUST TO SUPPLY-SIDE ECONOMICS: THE STRANGE HISTORY OF FEDERAL INTERVENTION IN THE ECONOMY

by

NAOMI LAMOREAUX

Naomi R. Lamoreaux is an Assistant Professor of History at Brown University.

DESPITE REPEATED PRONOUNCEMENTS THAT THE DAY OF strong Presidents is past, that the balance of power has shifted in favor of the Congress, within eight months of his inauguration Ronald Reagan won passage of the major components of his economic recovery program—massive tax cuts and budget cuts—notwithstanding the Democratic majority in the House. Reagan's success owed to his personal popularity and political shrewdness. But it was also the result of an extraordinary amount of public agreement about the direction federal policy should take. By the time of the 1980 election, most Americans had come to the conclusion that government itself was the major barrier to economic progress. Its large size had caused the economy to strain and groan under the burden. Moreover, along with large size went economic power—power that translated the whims of politicians into actions which wreaked havoc with the budgets and plans of Americans in all walks of life.

Loosely termed supply side economics, this extensive amount of agreement on economic policy is merely the most recent in a series of such consensuses that have occurred periodically and with varying levels of intensity throughout the 20th century: the antitrust movement of the Progressive Era, Franklin Roosevelt's early New Deal, Lyndon Johnson's Great Society. It is the purpose of this essay to trace the emergence and breakdown of these moods of public agreement with the aim of illuminating current events. For while the substantive content of these consensuses has varied enormously, all have had certain elements in common. Motivated by fear of economic power on the one hand and desire for economic security on the other, they have expressed the aspirations of individuals and groups whose interests would normally conflict. As a consequence, they carried within themselves the seeds of their own dissolution and depended for their persistence on a certain vagueness about the direction policy would actually take. When translated into concrete programs, the mood of consensus tended to dissolve and specific interests to reassert themselves. Nonetheless, while the consensus lasted the political atmosphere was unusually conducive to legislative activity. Thus, it is these periods that have put their mark on history; it is these periods when government's role in the economy has been most dramatically restructured.

The Progressive Era

In the early 20th century, the public demanded and received an expanded role for the federal government in the economy to counter the market power of big business. Before we can analyze this transformation, however, one important point must be made clear. While federal intervention in the economy was limited in the nineteenth century, other government activity was not. State and local agencies participated in economic life in many important ways: they promoted industrial expansion by means of tax breaks, loan guarantees, and even direct investment; set standards for the goods and services produced in their jurisdictions; and regulated the prices of basic commodities, conditions of factory labor, and railroad rates. In addition, states used their power to charter corporations to determine the very conditions under which incorporated enterprises could do business—the amount of capital they could raise, how much they could borrow, the types of production they could undertake, whether they could merge with other corporations.[1]

The extent of state and local activity rose and fell over the course of the 19th century, following a somewhat different time path in the different regions of the country. In general, high levels of intervention in the first half of the 20th century gave way to relatively low activity in the 1870s and early 1880s. But the formation of the Standard Oil Corporation in 1882 dramatically reversed the trend. Symbolizing both the concentration of economic power that was now possible and the potential that existed for abuse of that power, Standard Oil became the impetus for a major public outcry. The organization of similar combinations in the sugar, whisky, lead, linseed oil, cottonseed oil, cordage, and cattle industries made the clamor all the more insistent, and state officials moved to take action. In every region of the country states launched investigations, passed antitrust

---

[1] On the economic activities of state and local governments in the nineteenth century, see Jonathan R. T. Hughes, *The Governmental Habit: Economic Controls from Colonial Times to the Present* (New York: Basic Books, 1977); Louis Hartz, *Economic Policy and Democratic Thought, Pennsylvania, 1776-1860* (Cambridge: Harvard University Press, 1948); Oscar Handlin and Mary Flug Handlin, *Commonwealth: A Study of the Role of Government in the American Economy: Massachusetts, 1774-1861* (New York: New York University Press, 1947); Harry N. Scheiber, *Ohio Canal Era: A Case Study of Government and the Economy, 1820-1861* (Athens, OH: Ohio University Press, 1969).

On the use of states' charter powers, see Charles W. McCurdy, "The Knight Sugar Decision of 1895 and the Modernization of American Corporation Law, 1869-1903," *Business History Review*, LIII (Autumn 1979), pp. 304-42.

laws, and prosecuted combinations for violating either their antitrust laws, the common law, or the charters of constituent corporations.[2]

All this activity did not amount to much, however. While the states possessed the legal and political authority to act against the combinations, they lacked the economic power. Multi-plant giants whose enterprises were national in scope could respond to prosecution by shifting responsibility for the offending behavior to offices outside the state, by obtaining a charter from a more friendly jurisdiction, or even by closing down their enterprises in the state. The long depression of the 1890s made this last possibility all the more ominous, and states gradually softened their hostile stance.[3]

At the same time, however, the combination movement accelerated. Between 1895 and 1904 a great wave of mergers swept through the manufacturing sector. Unlike anything that has happened before or since, the Great Merger Movement featured the organization of numerous multi-firm consolidations that controlled major shares of the markets in which they operated. Approximately three thousand firms disappeared into mergers during these years. From half to two thirds joined combinations with market shares of 40 percent or better. At least 30 percent formed consolidations with more than 60 percent of their respective industries. Eleven percent merged into giants with market shares of over 80 percent.[4]

To contemporaries the merger movement was a terrifying phenomenon. Overnight, it seemed, the United States had been transformed from a nation of freely competing, individually owned enterprises into one dominated by a handful of giant corporations. Fearful of the power for abuse that large size threatened to grant, people agitated for something to be done.[5] Since state governments had already

---

[2]Alfred D. Chandler, Jr., *The Visible Hand: The Managerial Revolution in American Business* (Cambridge: Harvard University Press, 1977), pp. 315-339; Hans B. Thorelli, *The Federal Antitrust Policy: Origination of an American Tradition* (Baltimore: The Johns Hopkins Press, 1955), pp. 54-163; Charles W. McCurdy, *op. cit.*

[3]*Ibid*; Hans B. Thorelli, op. cit., pp. 235-368. States which controlled vital raw-material resources were an exception. For example, tough state antitrust laws effectively barred Standard Oil from the Texas oil fields in the early 20th century and facilitated the growth of new firms such as Texaco and Gulf. See Joseph A. Pratt, "The Petroleum Industry in Transition: Antitrust and Decline of Monopoly Control in Oil," *Journal of Economic History*, XL (December 1980), pp. 815-37.

[4]Ralph L. Nelson, *Merger Movements in American Industry, 1895-1956* (Princeton: Princeton University Press), pp. 100-03.

[5]We can follow precisely the course of public opinion, thanks to Louis Galambos's quantitative study of the attitudes towards big business expressed in several types of middle-class publications in this period. According to Galambos, negative sentiments toward big business attained an all-time high in the late 1890s when the trust movement overlapped the depression. Negative attitudes remained high in the early 20th century, then declined as the federal government assumed responsibility for regulating corporations. Louis Galambos, *The Public Image of Big Business in America, 1880-1940: A Quantitative Study in Social Change* (Baltimore: The Johns Hopkins Press, 1975), pp. 79-114.

proved themselves incapable of countering the economic power of large-scale corporations, the focus of attention shifted to Washington.

But what specifically should the federal government do? Despite the overwhelming sentiment for action, to which politicians of both major parties felt it necessary to respond, there was considerable disagreement about the direction federal policy should take. Since the divisions that developed among articulate spokesmen in this period persist in modified form to the present era, it is worth examining the debate in some detail.

Even among those in favor of federal antitrust action, opinion was divided.[6] One camp, whose ideas have been labeled the New Nationalism (the name attached to Theodore Roosevelt's platform in the 1912 campaign), held that large-scale combinations were the inevitable result of manufacturing innovations that raised the efficiency of production. For this reason combinations were not *per se* evil, but only if they abused the economic power that accompanied their large size. The proper goal of federal policy was to guard against this possibility — to regulate the actions of large corporations to insure that they observed the rules of fair play in dealing with competitors, consumers, suppliers, and labor.

Adherents of the other main position, which has been called the New Freedom (after Woodrow Wilson's platform in the same campaign), disagreed with the equation of large size and efficiency. Corporations had grown large, not as a result of productivity increasing innovations, but through the unfair and even illegal manipulation of market power — for example, extraction of freight rebates from railroads. As a consequence, the federal government had a responsibility to break up such ill-gotten concentrations of capital and to strengthen antitrust law and enforcement so as to prevent similar combinations from forming in the future.

Among businessmen, potential targets of federal regulation, there was also considerable difference of opinion about the direction antitrust policy should take. Although it is to this group that one must look for the source of opposition to federal intervention (especially since the antitrust movement was part of a many-faceted reform impulse, directed at, among other things, conditions in factories), at either end of the opinion spectrum business sentiment merged with the New Nationalist and New Freedom positions. At the New Freedom extreme, small businessmen lobbied for antitrust legislation that would help protect them against their larger competitors.[7] At

---

[6] Here I am using the categories that Ellis W. Hawley developed for his study, *The New Deal and the Problem of Monopoly: A Study in Economic Ambivalence* (Princeton: Princeton University Press, 1966), pp. 3-16.

[7] See Robert Wiebe, *Businessmen and Reform: A Study of the Progressive Movement* (Chicago: Quadrangle, 1962).

the New Nationalist end, officers of some of the nation's largest corporations (the most important was Judge Elbert H. Gary, Chairman of the United States Steel Corporation) welcomed federal intervention as an improvement over the confusing welter of state statutes. They also recognized that the federal government could serve as an important ally in their drive to stabilize business conditions in their industries.[8]

This debate over the purpose of federal economic policy was never resolved during the so-called Progressive period, but fear of the economic power of big business kept the antitrust issue alive. Politicians' response was to keep their rhetoric sufficiently vague to attract voters holding diverse opinions. Thus Wilson's New Freedom campaign at times sounded indistinguishable from Roosevelt's New Nationalism, and vice versa. Both candidates, moreover, sought to accommodate business voters.[9] Even the legislation that climaxed this period of reform activity was a model of vagueness. The Clayton Antitrust Act proscribed certain practices commonly acknowledged to be abuses of economic power, for example contracts for the sale or lease of a commodity imposing the condition that the purchaser or lessee "shall not use or deal in the goods...of a competitor...of the lessor or seller." But attached to this and other prohibitions was the qualifier, where the effect "may be to substantially lessen competition or tend to create a monopoly."[10] A companion law, the Federal Trade Commission Act, left to a quasi-judicial independent commission the interpretation of such controversial matters. How the antitrust laws would be enforced would depend on the composition of the commission.[11]

Hoover and Roosevelt

At this point World War I intervened. Antitrust activity was temporarily suspended, and government and business entered into close association to redirect production for the war effort. Partly as a result of this experience of cooperation, a new solution to the problem of big business emerged — one which lay the groundwork for broad agreement about the role of the federal government in the economy. Dubbed Associationism by historians, this solution was articulated most coherently by Herbert Hoover, who unceasingly promoted the

---

[8] See Gabriel Kolko, *The Triumph of Conservatism: A Reinterpretation of American History, 1900–1916* (Chicago: Quadrangle, 1963); James Weinstein, *The Corporate Ideal in the Liberal State, 1900–1918* (Boston: Beacon Press, 1968).

[9] Compare, for example, the conflicting statements by Woodrow Wilson reported in Gabriel Kolko, *op. cit.*, pp. 204–12; and in Arthur S. Link, *Woodrow Wilson and the Progressive Era* (New York: Harper Torchbooks-Harper & Row, 1963), pp. 20–22.

[10] F. M. Scherer, *Industrial Market Structure and Economic Performance* (2d ed.; Chicago: Rand McNally, 1980), pp. 494, 582.

[11] Interestingly, the first group Wilson appointed to the Commission consisted mainly of men with business backgrounds or pro-business records. Gabriel Kolko, *op. cit.*, pp. 270–71.

idea, first as Secretary of Commerce under Presidents Harding and Coolidge and then as President himself.[12]

The solution Hoover posed to the problem of big business was simple: give all economic actors the advantages of large size by encouraging them to form associations. If farmers joined together to form cooperatives, workers unions, and small businessmen trade associations, they would be able to pool resources for their common benefit and deal with big business on an equal footing. Take the case of small business, as an example. If the small firms that made up industries such as furniture or shoes were to form themselves into trade associations, they would gain market power in their dealings with large-scale enterprises. They would also be able to amass the capital necessary for national advertising and research and development—activities otherwise beyond the resources of all but the largest of the nation's businesses.

In Hoover's view, the role of government in an economy composed of associations would be limited. Although considerable help from government would be needed initially to promote the formation of unions, trade associations, and cooperatives, once the Associationist movement got underway, the role of government would be reduced. The government would simply collect and disseminate information to facilitate the smooth interaction of associations and serve as an umpire to insure that all groups adhered to the rules of fair play. Beyond that, the government might promote the stability of the entire system by planning public works expenditures so as to iron out the business cycle (undertaking construction projects during depressions and curbing government expenditures during booms), but such countercyclical spending was to be limited to strictly necessary projects.

The importance of Hoover's Associationist program cannot be underestimated—not because it was particularly successful, but because of the cravings for further government intervention which it awoke. The experience of the Cotton Textile Institute, the trade association in that industry, provides an excellent example. While the Institute successfully supervised the collection of funds for national advertising and research and development, it was not able to bring its members the market power they sought. Cotton textiles was a "sick" industry in the 1920s, characterized by severe competition,

---

[12] Hoover's image has undergone substantial revision since historians have gained access to his papers at the Herbert Hoover Presidential Library in West Branch, Iowa. For an excellent summary of the new research on Hoover's Associationist ideas, see J. Joseph Huthmacher and Warren I. Susman, ed., *Herbert Hoover and the Crisis of American Capitalism* (Cambridge, MA: Schenkman Publishing Co., 1973). See also Robert H. Zieger, "Herbert Hoover: A Reinterpretation," *American Historical Review*, 81 (October 1976), pp. 800–10.

falling prices, and declining profits (for the industry as a whole, profits were in fact negative for much of the decade). One of the motives for forming the Institute in the first place was to bring a measure of stability to the industry. But it soon became clear that the actions necessary to attain this goal (for example, sponsorship of industry-wide curtailments of production) brought the Institute dangerously close to violating federal antitrust laws. In order to succeed in stabilizing the industry, the Institute needed federal backing for industry-wide agreements to restrict production and maintain prices—in effect, a government-sanctioned cartel.[13]

In the case of the cotton textile industry, the government's encouragement of trade associations in the 1920s had awakened in manufacturers a craving for further government intervention. Cotton textiles was admittedly a sick industry in this period, but the same cravings developed in many other atomistic industries after the stock market crash of 1929. As slumping demand triggered outbreaks of price cutting, manufacturers clamored for relief—relief in the form of government-backed cartels. Proposals to suspend the antitrust laws and give trade associations the power to compel adherence to price and production restrictions were articulated in the early 1930s by prominent business leaders such as Gerard Swope of the General Electric Company, by a variety of trade associations, by the Chamber of Commerce, and by the American Bar Association. Bills embodying these proposals were introduced into Congress.[14]

Hoover's problem was that once he had awakened this craving for federal intervention, he was unwilling to satisfy it. It is well known that after the crash of 1929 Hoover refused to authorize relief expenditures on a scale sufficient to assuage popular demand. It is less well known that Hoover also refused to give in to business's pleas for help in curbing price declines. The Swope Plan and others like it, he ruled, were "the most gigantic proposal of monopoly ever made in history."[15] Voluntary cooperation in accordance with antitrust law was as far as Hoover would go; he was not willing to use the power of the federal government to police agreements to fix production and prices.[16]

But Franklin Roosevelt was. Again, it is well known that Roosevelt's relief efforts quickly surpassed those of Hoover. It is less well known that so did his efforts on behalf of business associations striving to restrain price competition. In fact, Roosevelt's early New Deal

---

[13]Louis Galambos, *Competition & Cooperation: The Emergence of a National Trade Association* (Baltimore: The Johns Hopkins Press, 1966), pp. 89-138.

[14]Ellis W. Hawley, op. cit., pp. 36-43.

[15]Quoted in *ibid.*, p. 42.

[16]See especially the essay by Robert F. Himmelberg in J. Joseph Huthmacher and Warren I. Susman, *op. cit.*, pp. 59-85.

was little more than the logical extension of Hoover's Associationist program.[17] The centerpiece of the early New Deal, the National Industrial Recovery Act (NIRA), set up machinery to organize firms in each industry into trade associations to write "codes of fair competition." Although Congress did not specify the content of the provisions to be included in the codes, the fact that the law specifically exempted the codes from the antitrust statutes suggests cartelization was the aim. Moreover, Congress granted the President unprecedented power to enforce the agreements: power to impose additional provisions, regulations, and fees; power to collect information from firms; power to institute licensing to prevent destructive wage and price cutting.[18]

The craving for federal intervention that Hoover's programs had awakened among businessmen had moved the nation toward consensus about the role of government in the economy. Roosevelt's contribution was to embody this consensus in a recovery program. Here his genius was essentially political, not economic, for Roosevelt assumed the Presidency without a clearly formulated plan for economic recovery. Although FDR busied Congress with a blitz of legislative proposals in his first month as President, his initiatives included no program for economic recovery — in large measure because Roosevelt was still unsure about the direction such a program should take. His stalling threatened to loosen his control of policy. On April 6, 1933, the Senate passed by a vote of 53 to 30 its own recovery mea-

---

[17] This point was made as early as 1935 by Walter Lippmann in "The Permanent New Deal," *Yale Review*, 24 (June 1935), pp. 649-67. See also William Appleman Williams, *The Contours of American History* (Chicago: Quadrangle, 1961), pp. 425-50; Barton J. Bernstein, "The New Deal: The Conservative Achievements of Liberal Reform," *Towards a New Past: Dissenting Essays in American History*, ed. by Barton J. Bernstein, (New York: Pantheon, 1968), pp. 263-88; Albert U. Romasco, "Hoover-Roosevelt and the Great Depression: A Historiographic Inquiry into a Perennial Comparison," *The New Deal: The National Level*, John Braeman, et al., (Columbus, OH: Ohio State University Press, 1975), pp. 3-26; Ellis W. Hawley, "The New Deal and Business," *ibid.*, pp. 50-82. See also the essays in J. Joseph Huthmacher and Warren I. Susman, *op. cit.*

[18] We know that groups in favor of cartelization, such as the Cotton Textile Institute, played a major role in drafting the legislation. See below. On the provisions of the Act, see Ellis W. Hawley, *The New Deal and the Problem of Monopoly, op. cit.*, pp. 31-33.

In accordance with Associationist principles, what Roosevelt did for business he also attempted to accomplish for labor and agriculture. Section 7A of the NIRA outlawed yellow dog contracts (contracts prohibiting membership in unions) and guaranteed workers the right to organize and to bargain collectively; other parts of the bill empowered the President to give the force of law to collective bargaining agreements. Agriculture received its own legislation, the Agricultural Adjustment Act, which encouraged cooperation and, like the NRA, brought to bear the power of the government on the side of agreements to restrict production and support prices. *Ibid.*, pp. 32-33, 191-92; William E. Leuchtenburg, *Franklin D. Roosevelt and the New Deal, 1932-1940* (New York: Harper Torchbooks-Harper & Row, 1963), pp. 48-52.

sure, a bill introduced by Senator Hugo Black of Alabama to mandate a 30-hour work week. In Roosevelt's view, Black's bill was unconstitutional, wrongheaded, and, even worse, politically divisive. Moving to take action to counter the Senator's proposal, he set three groups to work drafting an administration bill—one group under the leadership of Senator Wagner, known for liberal, pro-labor positions, one under General Hugh Johnson, who had played an important role mobilizing production for the war effort during World War I, and a third under John Dickinson, Assistant Secretary of Commerce. Ostensibly these groups represented different sectors of public opinion. They were to meet separately to draft legislative proposals and then join together to reconcile their differences and come out with a single bill. This was a technique Roosevelt would use time and again to insure that his legislation would have widespread appeal. What is remarkable in this case is how similar the groups' ideas were even as the drafting process began. Officials of the Cotton Textile Institute, for example, remained in close contact with, and had supporters among, members of all three committees. One of the writers in Wagner's group avowed support for the Institute's own proposal; Johnson personally consulted with the Institute, while Johnson's mentor, Bernard Baruch, assured its officials of his support; Dickinson voiced his agreement with the Chamber of Commerce proposal. Moreover, once their drafts were completed, the three groups were able to agree on a compromise bill in less than a week.[19]

Introduced in Congress on May 17, 1933, the National Industrial Recovery Act was quickly and overwhelmingly approved by the House (the vote that May 26 was 325-76). The bill ran into more difficulty in the Senate, which had already gone on record in favor of the Black Bill. But with the aid of an antitrust amendment (later dropped in conference), the bill passed the Senate by a vote of 58 to 24. Roosevelt signed the NIRA into law on June 16, 1933.[20]

The ease with which the various interests drafting the bill compromised with each other and the alacrity with which Congress acted are testimonies to the strength of the consensus about public policy that emerged in the early 1930s. Further evidence is provided by the eagerness with which the public embraced the program. The National Recovery Administration's logo, a blue eagle with the motto "We Do Our Part," suddenly appeared everywhere—pinned to clothing, affixed to shop windows. More than two million employers

---

[19]*Ibid.*, pp. 55-58; Louis Galambos, *op. cit.*, pp. 173-202; Ellis W. Hawley, *op. cit.*, pp. 21-26.
[20]*Ibid.*, pp. 30-31; William E. Leuchtenberg, *op. cit.*, p. 58.

signed a pledge to uphold NRA standards on wages and hours. A Blue Eagle parade in New York City drew a quarter of a million participants, making it the largest parade in the city's history.[21]

But the mood of consensus did not last for long. Once the code-writing process got underway, agreement over abstract matters of policy translated into conflict among interest groups over specific provisions of the codes. New Freedomites complained that businessmen were using the NRA to subvert the antitrust laws and monopolize their industries; New Nationalists felt the government was not taking a strong enough hand in formulating the codes; consumers griped that the end product of the codes was higher prices; labor protested that the government's promise of support for union organization and collective bargaining (embodied in Section 7A of the NIRA) was proving to be a chimera. Even business was unhappy. Within any given industry there was considerable disagreement about the rules of "fair competition." Weak firms wanted protection from the competition of their more vigorous rivals; strong firms, of course, desired to preserve their advantage. Disagreement even extended to provisions designed to improve efficiency in the industry as a whole. Some firms objected, for example, to provisions promoting standardization of commodities, because product differentiation constituted their main competitive weapon.[22]

By the time the Supreme Court declared the NIRA unconstitutional in the Schecter "sick chicken" case of 1935, the Act was already politically dead. The reasons are not difficult to understand. What the Act did, on the one hand, was substitute the public exercise of economic power for private and, on the other, transfer to the political arena basic allocational decisions formerly made by the market. It created a situation in which members of interest groups of all sorts sought to use political power in an attempt to raise their incomes above the level market forces had dictated. This was neither in the interests of recovery, nor politically feasible, and the entire program collapsed under the weight of contradictions.

Even if the political conflicts had been resolvable, the NIRA would likely have been an economic disaster. Events had substituted what was originally a solution to the problem of the economic power of big business for a solution to the problem of severe depression. Unfortunately, to the modern mind, the elements of the adopted solution were just the opposite of those needed to promote recovery. Even if the code-writing process had operated successfully, the end

---

[21] *Ibid.*, pp. 65–66.
[22] For a detailed account of conflict over NRA policy, see Ellis W. Hawley, *op. cit.*, pp. 53–129. See also Louis Galambos, op. cit., pp. 203–79; Arthur M. Schlesinger, Jr., *The Coming of the New Deal* (Boston: Houghton Mifflin, 1959).

result of government-sanctioned cartels would have been higher prices, lower production, and consequently lower employment than would otherwise have been the case — results that would have aggravated, not corrected, the disequilibrium of the economy.[23]

It is therefore perhaps fortunate that Roosevelt made no attempt to revive the NIRA after the Supreme Court handed down the Schecter decision in 1935. The political conflict which the codes had generated led Roosevelt to abandon the economic philosophy of the early New Deal and with it all hope of political consensus. Deliberately, FDR moved to the left. From this point on, he concentrated on building a strong base of support for the Democratic Party among the economically disadvantaged sectors of the population. This did not mean he abandoned the goal of recovery. Underpinning all his efforts on behalf of disadvantaged groups was a new theory of the causes of depression, one that attributed the nation's economic woes to structural flaws in the economy — in particular the maldistribution of income and wealth. Many of the legislative initiatives of the late New Deal — the Wagner Act, the Fair Labor Standards Act, the second Agricultural Adjustment Act, the Bankhead-Jones Farm Tenancy Act, the "soak-the-rich" taxes — can be seen as attempts to redress this imbalance. Of course, they also created deep political divisions between businessmen, on the one hand, and workers, farmers, and poorer sorts of people, on the other.[24]

It is beyond the scope of this essay to evaluate the programs of the late New Deal. One point needs to be made clear, however: Roosevelt, even at this stage, was not a Keynesian. While it is true that Roosevelt undertook massive expenditures for relief and that he financed some amount of these expenditures through deficit spending, it is also true that he remained a fiscal conservative, committed to the ideal of balancing the budget annually.[25] Whenever business conditions showed a hint of improvement, he would cut relief spending and throw recipients off the roles. As a result, the administration's relief efforts followed a cyclical pattern: cautious attempts to aid the poor and unemployed would give way to massive infusions of money as the conviction mounted that a major human emergency

---

[23] Ellis W. Hawley, *op. cit.*, pp. 130-35.

[24] On the late New Deal, see William E. Leuchtenberg, *op. cit.* For other views, see Paul K. Conkin, *The New Deal* (2d ed.; New York: Thomas Y. Crowell Co., 1975); Arthur M. Schlesinger, Jr., *The Politics of Upheaval* (Boston: Houghton Mifflin, 1960).

[25] Herbert Stein, *The Fiscal Revolution in America* (Chicago: University of Chicago Press, 1969), pp. 39-73, 91-130. After estimating the full-employment surplus for the 1930s, E. Cary Brown concluded, "Fiscal policy...seems to have been an unsuccessful recovery device in the 'thirties — not because it did not work, but because it was not tried." See "Fiscal Policy in the 'Thirties: A Reappraisal," *American Economic Review*, 46 (December 1956), pp. 857-79. See also Larry C. Peppers, "Full-Employment Surplus Analysis and Structural Change: The 1930s," *Explorations in Economic History*, 10 (Winter 1973), pp. 197-210.

was in the offing. Then as the mood of crisis subsided, expenditures would be cut back until the cycle began again.[26]

The last wave in this cycle began in late 1936 and early 1937. The economy seemed well on the road to recovery. Government revenues were increasing, partly as a result of the newly imposed social security payroll taxes, and Roosevelt determined to seize the opportunity to balance the budget. In 1937 he slashed federal spending, cutting funds for public works and throwing people off the relief roles. The cuts coincided with (some would say caused) the sharpest economic downturn in American history. Within months all the gains of the past two years had been lost. Some of Roosevelt's advisers, influenced by the writings of John Maynard Keynes, counseled an increase in government spending. After a long debate, Roosevelt agreed. A new spending package passed Congress in mid-1938. Perhaps coincidentally, the economy rebounded shortly thereafter.[27]

It was this conjunction of events plus the apparent stimulative effect of World War II—not Roosevelt's New Deal policy—that awakened among Americans an appreciation for Keynesian fiscal policy. In 1937 a sharp economic downturn had followed a cut in government expenditures; in 1938 the resumption of spending had seemed to turn the economy around. Moreover, massive infusions of purchasing power into the economy during World War II had accomplished virtually overnight what ten years of recovery legislation had failed to do: achieve full employment. As late as 1939, unemployment had hovered over 17 percent. Within a year of Pearl Harbor the rate had fallen to less than 5 percent and in 1943 to less than 2 percent.[28]

Post-War Keynesianism

What would happen when the war ended? As peace approached, anxiety mounted about the health of the economy after the war, and

---

[26]For example, Roosevelt's initial plans for relief were modest—the creation of a Civilian Conservation Corps (CCC). At the urgings of his cabinet he expanded his initiative and in 1933 sent a message to Congress which resulted in the establishment of the CCC, the addition of a public works program to the NIRA, and the creation of the Federal Emergency Relief Administration (FERA) to supervise a grant of $0.5 billion to the states. Roosevelt named Harold Ickes to head the public works program. Under Ickes's cautious leadership, the NIRA money trickled so slowly into the economy that it did little for relief. Harry Hopkins, the man FDR selected to head the FERA, was much bolder. Hopkins frightened Roosevelt with a forecast of the privation that would occur during the winter of 1933-34. With Roosevelt's approval, he set up the Civil Works Administration (CWA) and proceeded to create four million jobs in 30 days. Roosevelt, however, was horrified by the cost, the waste, the potential for corruption. As soon as spring came, he shut the program down. William E. Leuchtenberg, *op. cit.*, pp. 52-53, 70-71, 120-23.

[27]These events are typically depicted as cause and effect. For alternative explanations of the economy's ups and downs, see Herbert Stein, *op. cit.*, pp. 114-15. On the events of 1936-38, see *ibid.*, pp. 91-130; Ellis W. Hawley, *op. cit.*, pp. 383-410.

[28]U.S., Bureau of Economic Analysis, *Long Term Economic Growth, 1860-1970* (Washington, DC: Government Printing Office, 1973), p. 212.

with this anxiety grew the sentiment that government had a responsibility to safeguard prosperity and guarantee full employment. Yet this growing sentiment had not yet coalesced into a consensus on the specific direction federal policy should take. As the debate over the Employment Act of 1946 showed, most people agreed that full employment should be a national goal and that the government should guide the economy towards that goal. But there was considerable disagreement about the meaning of the term full employment, about the means government should use to achieve full employment, and whether attainment of full employment should take precedence over other goals. As a result, the Act which emerged from Congress in 1946 was a model of vagueness. It neither included the phrase full employment nor specified any particular government policy. Instead the Act merely instructed the federal government to use "all its plans, functions and resources" to maintain "maximum employment," leaving to the administration in power the task of determining what the law meant.[29]

In many respects, it was a situation reminiscent of that which had followed the Great Merger Movement of the turn of the century. A traumatic event (in that case the merger wave, in this case the depression) had created sentiment for a new role for the federal government in the economy. In both instances, there was widespread support for a shift in the government's role, but there was as yet little agreement about the precise form the new policy should take. Furthermore, in both cases the most active proponents of the new policy could be divided into two camps. By the end of World War II, heirs to the New Nationalist tradition supported Keynesian policy because it would improve their ability to manage the economy for the common good. Descendents of the New Freedom group perceived in Keynesian policy a means to pursue their antitrust goals without endangering the health of the economy. Once again, business groups constituted the main opposition to the new policy. The acrimonious relations between business and government that had developed by the time of Roosevelt's second administration had reawakened among businessmen a distrust of federal intervention in the economy. Of particular importance for the debate over Keynesian policy, Roosevelt's "soak-the-rich" tax proposals had convinced businessmen that the cost of an expansionary fiscal policy would fall most heavily on them.[30]

Nonetheless, there were from business's point of view several potential benefits to be derived from Keynesian policy. Business perceived that it had much to gain from a program that promised economic

---

[29]Herbert Stein, *op. cit.*, pp. 197–204.
[30]Ellis W. Hawley, *op. cit.*, pp. 270–80, 300–01, 350–51, 406–10; Hawley, "The New Deal and Business," *op. cit.*

stabilization—from the prosperity that it thought would obtain, of course, but also from elimination of the attacks on business that typically accompanied depressions. Further, Keynesian policy presented business with the intriguing possibility that government could intervene in the economy to insure prosperity without meddling in business's internal affairs. In contrast to all previous proposals for government intervention in economic life, this was a macro rather than a microeconomic program—and herein lay its attractiveness to business.[31]

It was the Eisenhower administration that made these benefits seem real to large segments of the business community. Here the Eisenhower administration played a role in the formation of Keynesian fiscal policy similar to that played by Hoover in the emergence of Associationism. Under Eisenhower business was reassured about the good intentions of the federal government, and a conservative version of Keynesian fiscal policy was introduced. Developed in the late 1940s by a group of businessmen working under the auspices of the Committee for Economic Development (CED), this conservative formulation became the official policy of the Eisenhower administration. The CED jettisoned the principle that government should attempt to balance the budget annually. Rather, government should exert countercyclical pressure on the economy by running deficits during recessions and surpluses during booms. The tax structure should be set with this goal in mind and should not be changed in response to business conditions—here the CED parted company with more liberal policy makers. A discretionary fiscal policy would not work, the CED argued, because changes in taxes and government spending were too cumbersome a response to changes in economic conditions. In the first place, they required approval by Congress; in the second, they were slow to take effect. To the extent that a discretionary policy was needed, the government should rely on monetary rather than fiscal tools for all but the most serious recessions.[32]

The Eisenhower administration adhered strictly to the CED's principles, but by the late 1950s doubts had surfaced as to the efficacy of this policy. Although the 1950s was ostensibly a decade of prosperity, the economy grew less rapidly than it had in any such period since the industrial revolution. The 2.7 percent annual rate of increase in real gross national product during Eisenhower's two terms was not sufficient to keep pace with the rate of growth of the labor force. Unemployment mounted from 3 percent in 1952 to 4.1 percent in the prosperous year 1956 to 6.8 percent during the recession in

---

[31] For an exhaustive treatment of business attitudes, see Robert M. Collins, *The Business Response to Keynes, 1929-1964* (New York: Columbia University Press, 1981).
[32] Herbert Stein, *op. cit.*, pp. 220-32, 281-308.

1958, and it remained at 5.5 percent in the subsequent recovery. Nor did this seem to be merely a business cycle phenomenon. Unemployment increased secularly; it averaged about 4 percent from 1950–1954, 5 percent from 1955–1958, 6 percent from 1959–1962.[33]

Most people agreed that the source of the problem was sluggish investment, especially in plant and equipment. Between 1950 and 1960 expenditures for plant and equipment had grown at a rate of only 2.3 percent per year, slower than the rate of growth of the economy as a whole, signifying that capital formation was accounting for a declining proportion of gross national product.[34] There was, of course, considerable debate about the causes of this development. Some analysts, especially representatives of the business community, argued that private investment was weak because industry was hamstrung by the high taxes and excessive regulations imposed by previous Democratic administrations. Others asserted that retardation in investment was the inevitable result of long-term developments such as the closing of the frontier, the decline in the rate of population growth, the relative increase in the size of the service sector, or the advent of mature capitalism.[35]

For proponents of one of these latter views, the message was clear. Private investment could no longer be counted on to propel the economy forward at a satisfactory rate of growth. The federal government had to step in and take up the slack. Rather than limiting itself to the worthy, though insufficient, goal of economic stabilization (the CED program), the government should take on the more comprehensive task of promoting economic growth. In the words of Walter Heller, who would be an architect of the new policy, "Nothing was more urgent than to raise the sights of economic policy and to shift its focus from the ups and downs of the cycle to the continuous rise in the economy's potential."[36]

The government could "raise the sights of economic policy" — could take up the slack in the economy — either, it was thought, by increasing government spending or by cutting taxes to stimulate consumption and investment spending. Since the latter option overlapped business's own remedy for sluggish investment, the elements of a new consensus on economic policy had emerged. As unemployment mounted, therefore, sentiment grew both for government to adopt a more active Keynesian policy and for government to cut taxes.

---

[33]*Ibid.*, pp. 309–71; U.S., Bureau of Economic Analysis, *op. cit.*, pp. 182–83, 212–13.
[34]*Ibid.*, *op. cit.*, pp. 186–87.
[35]Harold G. Vatter, *The U.S. Economy in the 1950s: An Economic History* (New York: W.W. Norton, 1963), pp. 282–94.
[36]Quoted in Jim F. Heath, *John F. Kennedy and the Business Community* (Chicago: University of Chicago Press, 1969), p. 33. See also James Tobin, *The New Economics One Decade Older* (Princeton: Princeton University Press, 1974), pp. 6–18.

These, however, Eisenhower refused to do. Once again the situation was a repetition—though admittedly lacking much of the same sense of urgency—of the events of the late 1920s and early 1930s. Like Hoover before him, Eisenhower held firm amidst accelerating demands that he take his policy to its logical extension. Just as Hoover's Associationism had helped make respectable the idea of federal microeconomic intervention, so Eisenhower's acceptance of the CED program did macroeconomic. Yet Eisenhower was unwilling to satisfy the cravings for more extensive federal intervention that his policy awoke.

A similar refusal had cost Hoover the 1932 election; Eisenhower's steadfastness helped defeat Nixon in 1960. In 1933 Roosevelt had assumed office ready to take Hoover's Associationist policies to their logical extension; now Kennedy did the same for Eisenhower's conservative version of Keynesian economics. Kennedy's contribution was to sense the possibility for consensus that underlay business's desire for tax cuts and the growing recognition that it was necessary to stimulate investment spending. Since, unlike Roosevelt, Kennedy did not operate under conditions of national emergency, he proceeded cautiously to lay the political groundwork for his stimulus policy. Legislation was in the works in 1963 when Kennedy was assassinated; it was left to Johnson to guide the bill through its final stages in early 1964.[37]

It is interesting to note that Kennedy's program of economic stimulus took the form of a deep across-the-board tax cut similar to that recently enacted by the Reagan administration. Though the substance of Kennedy's legislation was similar to Reagan's, the justification for it at the time was completely different from that offered today. Kennedy's tax cut program was formulated and perceived as the positive act of a government operating under the assumptions of Keynesian economics. Administration officials had diagnosed the economy as operating below its potential. They had then calculated the size of the tax cut needed to generate sufficient consumption and investment spending to close the gap. A tax cut was the correct medicine for the economy in the early 1960s, they believed, but under other circumstances curing the economy's ills might require a tax increase, or more or less government spending. Thus the tax cut of 1964 was perceived not as a move toward less government involvement in economic life, but simply as a particular form of government intervention.[38]

It is necessary to realize that the tax cut was perceived as the positive

---

[37]*Ibid.*, pp. 1–47, 114–29; Herbert Stein, *op. cit.*, pp. 319–453.

[38]*Ibid.*, pp. 372–84; Tobin, *op. cit.*, pp. 18–27.

act of an activist government in order to understand what happened in its aftermath. To the gratification of Johnson and his advisers, the tax cut worked like a charm. The economy seemed to take off. GNP rose 6.3 percent between 1964 and 1965 and 6.5 percent between 1965 and 1966.[39] The lesson that was drawn from this growth spurt was not the one that would be drawn today: that the economy performed better when burdened less by government. Rather the success of the tax cut, interpreted as it was within the framework of Keynesian analysis, generated an extraordinary optimism about the federal government's ability to manage the economy for the common good.

It is difficult today to imagine the extent of this optimism. Government experts had diagnosed the ills of the economy, had proposed solutions, and had applied them successfully. The cure had worked. Why not, then, shift the focus of attention to other economic diseases such as poverty? The means were at the nation's disposal. All that was required was to switch the stimulus program from tax cutting to government spending. Just direct the increased expenditures to the elimination of poverty and other evils, and the Great Society was within reach.[40]

The problem was, however, that this involved once again a confusion of goals. Where Roosevelt had, with the passage of the NIRA, substituted a solution to the problem of economic power for a solution to the problem of recovery, Johnson did just the reverse. In this case, moreover, the substitution was particularly disastrous because the idea that economic growth could be stimulated by government spending was based on a (to the present mind) misunderstanding of how the economy functions. If one envisions the economy as represented by a simple supply and demand diagram, the argument reduces to a debate over the shape of the aggregate supply curve — whether it is upward sloping or vertical. The justification for an expansionary fiscal policy rests on the assumption that the aggregate supply curve is upward sloping — that is, an increase in government spending shifts the aggregate demand curve upward so that it intersects the aggregate supply curve at a point where both prices and output are higher than before. If the aggregate supply curve is upward sloping, then, there is a trade-off between inflation and economic growth. If, on the other hand, one assumes that the aggregate supply curve is vertical, the effect of an upward shift in the aggregate demand curve is to raise prices but not output. There is, under this assumption, no trade-off between inflation and growth.

---

[39]U.S., Bureau of Economic Analysis, *op. cit.*, pp. 182–83; Tobin, *op. cit.*, p. 34.

[40]See, for example, Doris Kearns, *Lyndon Johnson and the American Dream* (New York: Harper & Row, 1976), pp. 210–14.

Keynesian economists suggested a number of theoretical justifications for the assumption that the aggregate supply curve is upward sloping, but one by one these have been demolished by other economists. The last of the justifications to remain undemolished was the concept of money illusion.[41] According to the Keynesian argument, whenever prices rise (as, for example, when an increase in government spending shifts the aggregate demand curve upward), some economic actors (say workers) fail to perceive that the increase in prices affects their real income. They do not demand a corresponding increase in nominal wages. As a consequence, real wages fall, more labor is hired, and national product increases. So long as money illusion persists, the effect of an increase in government spending is higher employment and greater output.

Other economists acknowledge that money illusion may affect economic actors in periods when rises in the general price level are infrequent or small. Once, however, repeated increases in government spending generate repeated rounds of price increases, people are likely to get smart. Workers, to continue the example, will demand that their nominal wages keep pace with inflation. To the extent that they are successful in achieving their demands, real wages will not fall as the price level rises, the stimulus to additional employment will disappear, and the effect of an increase in spending will simply be a rise in prices — not output and employment.

Such an eventuality seems in fact to have resulted from the growth in government spending that accompanied Lyndon Johnson's Great Society and especially his waging of the Viet Nam war. Repeated rises in government spending stimulated corresponding increases in prices which in turn moved economic actors to seek ways to protect their income from erosion by inflation. As a consequence, the terms of the trade-off between growth and inflation worsened severely. Policy makers found themselves in a bind. When the economy's rate of growth began to decline again and unemployment to rise, there was little they could do to reverse the trend. Now that economic actors no longer suffered from money illusion, injections of government spending produced inflation but little or no additional employment and output. The economy had entered an era of "stagflation."

Supply Side Economics

The way out of the bind is implicit in the supply and demand apparatus described above: change strategy and concentrate on shifting, not the aggregate demand curve, but the aggregate supply curve.

---

[41] Mark Blaug, *Economic Theory in Retrospect* (3d ed.; Cambridge: Cambridge University Press, 1978), pp. 665–96. For a technical discussion of the concept of money illusion, see the accompanying essay by David Tuerck.

Hence the term supply side economics. This solution was obvious to many policy makers by the early 1970s, but, as might be guessed from the argument developed in this essay so far, there was little agreement about the best way to go about increasing aggregate supply. For some theorists, heirs once again to the New Freedom position, the problem was the degree of monopoly power in the American economy. In order to protect investments in existing plant and equipment, big business used its market power to stifle technological innovation and the expansion of output. At the same time, its control over prices aggravated inflation. Only by aggressively enforcing the nation's antitrust laws, by preventing large firms from abusing their economic power, by breaking up the worst offenders, could aggregate supply be increased.[42] For other policy makers, descendents of the New Nationalists, the solution to the problem of stagflation was government planning—a carefully structured system of incentives and disincentives that would direct the reallocation of the nation's resources from less to more productive uses.[43] While the New Nationalists proposed more government intervention as a solution to the country's economic woes, others, including many businessmen, perceived the root of the problem to be the government itself. In the first place, the expansionary fiscal policy of the federal government had caused the size of the annual budget to grow, creating a heavy tax burden and high rate of inflation that retarded investment in plant and equipment. Second, the increase in the regulatory functions of government that had occurred steadily throughout the 20th century had destroyed business initiative and diverted the allocation of the nation's resources away from their most productive uses.[44]

The history of the 1970s is the tale of growing consensus around the last of these three positions. The direction of this shift in public opinion, therefore, marks a sharp break with the past. In similar periods earlier in the century the movement toward consensus had been characterized by growing acceptance on the part of businessmen of a stronger role for government in the economy—either to guard against the private exercise of economic power or to guarantee economic stability. By the 1970s, however, this succession of consensuses had resulted in an enormous expansion in the federal government's role in the economy, increasing both the government's size and its economic power. At this point there was a reversal in the

---

[42] See, for example, Gardiner Means, *et al.*, *The Roots of Inflation: The International Crisis* (New York: Burt Franklin & Co., 1975), especially the essay by Means.

[43] This is essentially Lester Thurow's proposal in *The Zero-Sum Society: Distribution and the Possibilities for Economic Change* (New York: Basic Books, 1980).

[44] See the other essays in this volume, especially the articles by Norman Ture and David Raboy.

trend. Americans increasingly perceived the government's large size to be a burden on the economy, an obstacle to the attainment of stability that government expansion had originally aimed to achieve. In addition, the exercise of economic power by the government now seemed to pose a greater threat to individual enterprise than the big businesses government power sought to counter. Events of the late 1960s and early 1970s drove this message home. The government's persistence in waging an unpopular war, the revelations in the Pentagon Papers, and the long, drawn-out Watergate investigations suggested the potential for abuse of power by the federal government. The threat posed by big business paled in comparison.

With these developments, the New Freedom position, directed as it was at the economic power of big business, lost its cogency. The New Nationalist argument, which assumed that benevolent central planning by the federal government was possible, also lost much of its appeal. Remaining were business's proposals for deregulation and less government spending. All that was needed, then, to complete the formation of a consensus was for large sectors of the American public to adopt this last position as their own.

Now the Carter administration played a role similar to that of the Hoover and Eisenhower administrations in providing the catalyst for the formation of a consensus. Carter ran for office on an anti-government platform. He lectured the American people that big government was at the root of the nation's economic problems. He promised to streamline the bureaucracy and thereby reduce its burden on the economy and on taxpayers, while at the same time making the government function more efficiently. He also promised to maintain the Democratic Party's traditional commitment to programs for the poor and disadvantaged. In reality he was unable to accomplish all these tasks. The government apparatus was not effectively streamlined under his administration, the burden on taxpayers went unreduced, the nation's economic problems unsolved. Since Carter himself had helped give credence to the idea that big government was responsible for the nation's economic woes, the response to his failure was to demand greater cuts in government spending. In addition, some of the actions that the Carter administration took to reduce government intervention in the economy—for example, the deregulation of petroleum prices—undermined the living standards of people who formed the rank and file of the Democratic Party, communicating to these traditional supporters of big-government policies that the exercise of economic power by the federal government could be a dangerous thing.

This growing fear of the economic power of the federal government plus the conviction that big government was at the root of the economy's problems formed the consensus that gave Ronald Reagan his mandate in the 1980 election. Hence when he assumed the Presidency, Reagan was in a position similar to Roosevelt in the 1930s and Kennedy in the 1960s. All three Presidents were the beneficiaries of a gradual shift in public opinion about the role of government in the economy. All three were also the beneficiaries of the policies of a predecessor of the opposite party, who helped make the new ideas palatable to groups most likely to be in the opposition.

If Reagan is in a position similar to that of these earlier Presidents, what does their experience tell us is likely to occur in the near future? Since the new consensus, like those in the past, brings together groups with interests that would normally conflict, it is likely that the consensus will begin to dissolve as the supply side rhetoric is translated into concrete policies. Indications are that this is already happening. Reagan is having much more difficulty getting his programs through Congress than he did at the beginning of his administration. If the trend persists and the consensus breaks up further, Reagan may behave in a manner similar to Roosevelt. Where FDR abandoned all hope of consensus and moved to the left to build a new base for the Democratic Party, Reagan may move further to the right.

But it is not at all certain that the consensus will continue to break up. If Reagan's supply side economics works, if it stimulates economic growth and reduces inflation, then conflict among different groups in the consensus will be minimized, and the Reagan administration's stake in maintaining the center coalition will continue. Past policies foundered in part because government officials misapplied solutions to the problem of economic power to the problem of economic growth and stability, or vice versa. Supply side economics, by contrast, claims to be a solution to both types of problems. To the extent that these claims are correct, this policy's chances for longevity are enhanced.

HB 241 .E847 1982

Essays in supply side
economics /